# INTENT TO PROSPER

Ashley —
Live long and prosper!

Love,
Daddy

# INTENT TO PROSPER

## Vol. 1

### Commercial Real Estate

R. Kymn Harp

Cover photo courtesy of Steven Dahlman Photography

Library of Congress Control Number: 2008909391
ISBN:  Hardcover  978-1-4363-7920-5
Softcover  978-1-4363-7919-9

This book was printed in the United States of America.

To order additional copies of this book, contact:
Xlibris Corporation
1-888-795-4274
www.Xlibris.com
Orders@Xlibris.com
38661

# CONTENTS

*Dedicated to Aunt Sophie*

*Also dedicated to*
*Margaret, Earl and Ryan Harp, Ken and Ashley Klotz,*
*Christopher and Ashley Podraza, and to*
*Kery, my dear departed wife*

*Special thanks to*
*Rose Rosario Quiles, Dr. Severko Hrywnak,*
*Deborah Knupp, James A. Regas, James and Meira Mainzer,*
*Bea Klain, James M. Palazzo, LeoDeGario Lopez, Cynthia V. Gonzalez,*
*Noshir R. Daruwalla, Laura Lau Marinelli, Jennifer Hollenbeck Sarhaddi,*
*Tim Gray, Azam Nizamuddin, James A. Chatz and Dr. John Kotis*

# Introduction

There are a lot of ways to make money. Commercial real estate is one of them. Since you have picked up this book, it's a good bet commercial real estate is where you plan to make yours. Good choice. There is big money to be made in commercial real estate.

I grew up in a real estate family and have been a commercial real estate lawyer for over thirty years. I've learned a lot during that time. Among the lessons I've learned is that developers and high-end commercial real estate investors are a breed all their own.

When I say I "grew up in a real estate family," what I mean is that investing in real estate was always a topic of conversation. My parents invested in real estate. My grandparents invested in real estate. My uncle Bob and his family invested in real estate. My cousins invested in real estate. Growing up, I thought every family did. On my mother's side of the family, it was mostly residential real estate. On my father's side of the family, it was mostly commercial real estate. I was surprised at the stir it caused among my friends and their families when I bought my first rental property at age sixteen. I thought everyone invested in real estate.

I soon discovered my family was not like most others. While we were discussing real estate, they were thinking about cars and boats and swimming pools. Not that there is anything wrong with that. We had those things too. It's just that in my family, real estate and investing were almost always an integral part of our dinner table conversation. It is in our blood.

I learned early on that what I take for granted as common knowledge is not always as common as I sometimes believe. That discovery has been reinforced as I have begun over the past few years to write articles about commercial real estate and have presented seminars on various real estate-related topics. I started doing this because I thought it would be a good way to grow my law practice. Through the feedback I receive, I am continually reminded that what appears obvious to me is sometimes news to my clients, colleagues, and friends.

For me, it's a kick. I get to share what I have learned about real estate investing, development, and financing by telling real-life stories I have been fortunate to experience. People actually pay me to pursue my passion. It reminds me of when I was a kid playing bass guitar in blues-rock bands (now considered *classic rock*). I get to do what I love and get paid for it. Cool.

I am aware that, to some, talking about real estate investment is about as enjoyable as going to the dentist. I say that with apologies to my close friend, Dr. William Mark Standring, who happens to be a very successful dentist in my hometown. I am sure he understands. He has made more than a few bucks investing in real estate himself.

I've known Mark since high school. We played in a successful rock band together. Mark was the drummer. We have been close friends ever since. With our common background, Mark and I share a similar approach to life. We are serious about what we do professionally, but we want to have fun and want those interacting with us to have fun as well. Mark does what he does on land, sea, and air. He is a man for all seasons.

My life is a bit more reserved largely because my passion is also my work. In all events, when I practice law and write about commercial real estate, I try to keep it light and interesting. Hopefully, that's how you will find this book. There are serious lessons to be learned, but I believe they can be learned without resorting to textbook drudgery.

Playing in rock bands in Evansville, Indiana, in the mid to late 1960s must have triggered some sort of success gene, with an emphasis on real estate and business. Besides Mark Standring's success, Alan Graf, the first drummer I ever practiced bass guitar with, became CFO of Federal Express. Victor Lopez, a guitarist in two iterations of an early rock band, became senior vice president of development for Hyatt Corporation. Mark Bethel, our High Tides convert, played keyboards and became a commercial real estate developer with General Growth Corporation in Chicago before leaving to found the Henderson Project in Henderson, Kentucky. He then became a principal in Bethel Parrish Skinner, a predevelopment company focusing on master planning for urban development, and director of development for Nakheel Retail where he is currently responsible for development and planning of over 15 million square feet of retail space. I've lost track of the others, but clearly, something special happened in those rock band days that seems to have affected all of us in a positive way.

This book will not teach you everything you need to know about commercial real estate. There is always more to learn. But if you are serious about investing in, developing, or financing commercial real estate, you do need to know much of what is in this book.

# 1

# Why Commercial Real Estate?

It is estimated that in the United States alone, over $400 *billion* dollars in commercial real estate transactions occur each year.

The commercial real estate industry is huge and multifaceted. The vast majority of all business is conducted in or from commercial real estate. It touches all aspects of human experience. Even the virtual world of e-commerce relies on commercial real estate to manufacture and house its servers, computers, and other hardware; to provide offices for software designers and users; to warehouse merchandise being offered through the Internet; and to provide countless other commercial uses.

The commercial real estate industry, as I have come to define it, encompasses all nonfarm, nonresidential real estate held for investment or for use in a trade or business. Although residential property is generally excluded, the commercial real estate industry is often defined to include multifamily housing held out for rent and, from the viewpoint of the developer, residential condominium projects developed and offered for sale to the public. Farm operations are clearly a commercial enterprise, but farmland investment is a unique category all its own and is therefore excluded from my definition of commercial real estate. Similarly, single-family homes and condominiums, though sometimes acquired and held out for rental to consumers, are excluded as well. They may be investment

1

real estate, but are not considered commercial real estate. Some of the same lessons apply, but they have distinct issues which are not applicable to commercial real estate generally.

Commercial real estate is divided into subcategories, each with its own subset of characteristics and unique challenges. There are retail shopping centers and freestanding retail stores, office buildings, sports and entertainment venues, restaurants, banquet facilities, nightclubs, hotels, casinos, gas stations, banks, health care facilities, warehouses, logistics terminals, distribution centers, industrial and manufacturing facilities, pay-to-park parking lots and parking garages, golf courses, resorts, and other specialty categories. In many cases, a single development may be a mix of several categories of use, such as a mixed-use development with retail stores, offices, a pay-to-park parking garage, a restaurant or entertainment venue, hotel and residential apartments or condominiums all in the same building or project.

You do not need to be Donald Trump or his remarkable daughter Ivanka to get involved in commercial real estate. There are many opportunities to make your mark and collect your profit. If you are interested in commercial real estate but can't find a place to fit in, you aren't looking hard enough.

The industry is so large and all-encompassing it is not possible for a single person to know everything there is to know about commercial real estate. Consequently, people tend to specialize in a particular aspect of commercial real estate and rely on others to provide the specialized knowledge they don't have. This is an important point to note. Even the most savvy investors and developers seldom go it alone. Commercial real estate investment and development is a team sport.

As large as the commercial real estate industry is, it is also one of the most decentralized industries in the world. You don't need to be a shopping center developer or build skyscrapers to profit in the industry. The individual who buys or builds a single building to use or rent out as an office or store or warehouse or other commercial use is participating in the commercial real estate industry. Commercial real estate properties can range in price and value from less than $100,000 to several hundred millions, and even billions, of dollars.

To prosper in commercial real estate, you have to decide where you intend to fit in, make a decision to do so, then act in a purposeful way to carry out your decision. Sounds simple, right? It's easier than you think, but not quite as easy as it sounds.

# 2

# The Profit Motive

This book is for current or prospective developers, investors, brokers, lenders, owners, and sellers of commercial real estate. It should also be read by, and perhaps *especially* be read by, their attorneys. But first things first: to get a clear picture of what we need to know, we must first admit why we are getting into the field of commercial real estate.

This seems obvious, but experience shows the obvious must sometimes be stated. We are not getting into commercial real estate predominantly because we want to make the world a better place in which to live. We may want that, but that is not our primary motivation. We are interested in participating in the commercial real estate industry because we want to make money—lots of money. That is the *why* for all of us. There is not a single person actively involved in buying, selling, leasing, financing, or developing commercial real estate who does not do so primarily to make money. That is the motivation. That is the goal. That is the overriding objective. Anyone who tells you differently is lying.

We need to accept this for at least two reasons. Number one, we need to let go of any embarrassment this admission may cause. We must acknowledge it. Making money is the real and primary reason we are interested in commercial real estate. This admission may be harder for those of us who came of age in the antimaterialism environment of the mid to late 1960s, but get over it. We want to make money. We are trying to make a profit. Not just a little profit, we want to make *big* money. We want to prosper.

The other reason we need to accept our profit motive is to give us an objective standard by which to calculate our investment decisions. In my professional life, I have seen otherwise savvy investors, time and again, get emotionally attached to a particular property or project that makes little economic sense. It becomes their dream. Their crowning glory. It strokes their ego. It may also be their financial undoing.

My family has a saying: "If it is not a 'good deal,' it is not a *good* deal." Translation: if you are not objectively certain (as certain as one can be in any investment decision) that you will make an acceptable profit, the deal is not worth doing. Walk away. We are in this business to make money, not to stroke our egos.

Say it to yourself. Post a sign on your door. Repeat it often. "If it is not a 'good deal,' it is *not* a *good* deal." (I should sell bumper stickers.)

With that in mind, we must ask ourselves, How do we know we have a *good* deal? What do we need to do to make money in commercial real estate?

First and foremost, we need to decide what precisely it is we want to accomplish. Where do we fit in? What will be our role? Then we need to figure out what we need to know to fulfill our chosen objective.

It is not enough to simply want to make money in commercial real estate. That is not a precise-enough objective to make it happen. It is certainly more specific than a general statement that you simply *want to make a lot of money*—at least you have narrowed the universe down to the field of commercial real estate, but the commercial real estate industry is vast.

What precisely do you intend to do? How will you fit in? What is your niche?

Are you going to be a developer? Investor? Commercial real estate broker? Leasing agent? Environmental consultant? Financial analyst? Architect? Appraiser? Commercial real estate attorney? Tax advisor? Project manager? Mortgage banker? Commercial lender? Fund underwriter? Other? (If *other*, what other?)

If you are going to be an investor or developer, what type of properties are you going to invest in or develop? Strip shopping centers? Individual retail stores? Regional malls? Outlet power centers? Restaurant buildings? Medical buildings? Multifamily housing? Office buildings? Mixed-use developments? Marinas? Hotels? Industrial warehouses? Private airports? Logistics terminals? Parking lots and parking garages? Distribution centers? Sports and entertainment arenas? Other?

Are you going to concentrate on investment in and development of undeveloped open areas and farmland, generally referred to as "greenfield development"? Redevelopment of environmentally challenged property, generally referred to as "brownfield development"? Redevelopment, conversion, and recycling of blighted and functionally obsolete urban properties, generally referred to as "infill development"? Redevelopment, restoration, and preservation of historic properties? Development of low- to medium-income housing? Development of luxury apartments and condominiums?

You have to figure out where you are going to put your energy and then learn everything you need to know about the specific type of development or investing you intend to pursue. Rarely can one person do it all and do it all well.

Are you going to rely primarily on your own money and conventional financing? Other investors? Seller financing? Sale and leaseback financing? Capital markets? Government incentives and entitlements? A combination of sources?

When you have selected a particular project, how will you analyze the project and the investment or development issues it presents? How will you know you can use it in the way you envision? How will you finance it? How will you evaluate if you can make a sufficient economic return to justify the necessary commitment of your time, energy, and resources?

One of the most common- and wrong-statements you will hear about real estate investing is the platitude "There is only a limited amount of real estate and an ever-growing population. The law of supply and demand means you can't lose money investing in real estate." Sounds good, but it's not true.

There are ample examples of real estate investments that have lost money. Ask any experienced investor or developer. Market conditions change. Assumptions turn out to be incorrect. Interest rates jump up. Necessary zoning and entitlements can't be obtained. You name it. If it can go wrong, it will. Murphy's law is alive and well in the commercial real estate industry.

Just consider the economic pause we have experienced in the commercial real estate market during 2007 and 2008. It is very likely to extend into 2009 and perhaps beyond. If not for that pause (and it is just a pause), I would not likely have included in this book the two chapters on *loan workouts*. Investors and lenders new to the industry may think this is the end of the commercial real estate world. It is not. Commercial real estate will rebound. It must. It is essential to our way of life. If properly positioned, investors active in the market today will make a fortune in the next three to ten years. Where there are losers, there are winners. But in the short run, you can lose your shirt investing in and financing commercial real estate if you don't know what you are doing. To survive

7

a down market, you need staying power, a realistic understanding of the economic horizon, the vision to see past that economic horizon, and knowledge of commercial real estate fundamentals. With these, you will be well positioned to catch hold of and ride the next bull market in commercial real estate when it comes. Believe me, it is coming. If you don't believe me, put down this book. It will be of little use to you. Get out of the race and take your position on the sideline.

There is a saying, "In a race, everyone runs. Only the winner gets the prize." To be a winner in commercial real estate takes knowledge and insight.

So what will you do when deciding on your next project? Will you just assume the risk and hope for the best? Rely on your *instincts*? Tell yourself that you are luckier or smarter than everyone else—that they *just don't get it* like you do?

What evidence do you have to support that claim? There are a lot of smart people in commercial real estate. What is it that distinguishes your approach to commercial real estate investment that will make you one of the winners?

Commercial real estate is not a game of chance—or at least it should not be. Certainly, there are risks and factors you cannot eliminate or control, but there are many you can. To prosper, you need to discover and eliminate those risks within your power to eliminate and minimize the potential damage caused by risks you cannot eliminate. Unfortunately, there is always the risk of unknown and unknowable factors. Your job is to discover, then eliminate or control, as many of the knowable risks as possible.

Fortunately, in commercial real estate, there is an ordered process for discovering potential risks in any given transaction or real estate development. The process is known as due diligence. Due diligence is, in fact, not really a process, but rather a standard of conduct. What is referred to as the due diligence process is actually a focused investigation of the facts and circumstances surrounding a proposed investment or development decision using that degree of diligence due and appropriate under the circumstances of that particular case. We will talk more about that later.

# 3

# The Threshold Decision:
# Specific Intent

We have agreed that our overall objective is to make a profit and prosper. That is what we want. But understand, wanting something and developing the specific intent to have it are two distinctly different things.

Merely wanting something won't get it done. You have to make a decision. You have to decide specifically that you intend to prosper though your chosen path in commercial real estate, and then you have to take intentional steps to fulfill that objective. Acting with intentionality will not necessarily guaranty success, but acting without the specific intent to accomplish a specific objective will almost certainly end in failure. Real estate fortunes are seldom made by accident.

Once you adopt the specific intent to follow a particular path in the commercial real estate industry and commit yourself to doing whatever is necessary to fulfill that objective, your course of action will begin to define itself. Not everything you need to learn or do may be immediately clear, but once your definitive decision is made, you will start down a path of discovery and accomplishment that will take you where you have decided to go.

With my kids, I illustrate this point by making an analogy to going on vacation. If you simply say you want to go on vacation, you are virtually nowhere along the path of doing so. If you say you want to go on vacation in a warm climate, on a beach, for two weeks, you are getting closer. But if you decide, specifically, that you intend to go on vacation the last two weeks of next February and stay at a beach resort in the Riviera Maya, Mexico, with golf available during the day and an active club scene close at hand at night, you will have established the specific criteria necessary to act. Your path to fulfilling your decision is made clear. You will see clearly that you need to research available resorts that meet your established criteria, find the means to pay for your vacation, book the travel and resort accommodations, make arrangements to take that time off from work, obtain a passport if you don't already have one, pack your bags, and go. Oh, and by the way, pack sunscreen and have a great time.

What makes this work is the specific intent to accomplish a specific objective, coupled with the willingness to do what must be done to actually fulfill the objective. Merely expressing a general *want* is not enough. That is why merely saying you *want to make a lot of money in commercial real estate* is not specific enough. It is like wanting to go on vacation without having made a specific decision as to where, when, or how. General *wants* are meaningless.

I *want* to learn how to play the piano. I *want* to learn how to speak Spanish. I *want* to be in great physical shape. Wanting these things is not enough. In order to accomplish any of these things, I would need to make a specific decision to do so and would need to commit to taking the necessary steps and committing the necessary time and effort to make it happen. I am certain I have the mental capacity to learn Spanish and to play the piano if I decided to commit myself to doing so. If I really desired to improve my physical condition, I could improve my diet and work out every day. The fact is, however, I want these things in a general way; but I have not made a decision to actually do any of them. Maybe I will someday—but not today. They would interfere with what I have specifically decided to do today, which is write this book.

# 4

# Specific Intent to Invest in Real Estate

As a commercial real estate lawyer, it is fairly common for me to have friends, clients, or acquaintances tell me they would like to invest in commercial real estate. The conversation usually goes something like this: "Kymn, you must see a lot of deals. We should do a project together. The next time a really good deal comes across your desk, let me know." To that I may respond, "What kind of real estate project are you interested in? What geographic area? What price range? What rate of return do you need? Are you willing to redevelop, or are you looking for an existing turnkey operation?" Often the reply is something like, "Oh, anything would be fine. Just find me a good deal."

I can tell you from experience that this kind of exchange is common and is simply small talk. These people *want* to invest in real estate but have no specific intent to do so. It is simply not likely to happen. This kind of *want* is even less specific than me saying I want to learn Spanish. It's more like someone saying, "I'd like to learn a foreign language," but they haven't even decided which one yet.

Now, compare that conversation to this one that actually occurred: One day a client walked into my office and said, essentially, "Kymn. I want to buy and redevelop the Marina City Commercial Complex in downtown

Chicago and turn it into a mixed-use entertainment center." Now that is specific intent. The client was my friend John L. Marks, of Mark IV Realty Group in Chicago.

When John walked into my office on that day in 1992 to announce his specific intent to acquire and redevelop the Marina City Commercial Complex, he didn't know exactly how he was going to accomplish his goal. The owner was in bankruptcy. The property was burdened with nearly $10 million in past due real estate taxes. It was largely vacant and decaying. And the owners of the condominium units on the top forty floors of the two landmark corncob-shaped towers wanted nothing to do with any developer, having been burned by broken promises of redevelopment in the past. To complicate matters further, the property had been in foreclosure prior to bankruptcy, with a receiver appointed who claimed a priority lien against the property. The city of Chicago had filed suit complaining of numerous building code violations. And once John made known his vision to acquire and redevelop the complex, a competing developer tried to step in and take the project away through the bankruptcy court's competitive bidding process.

The obstacles facing John as he sought to redevelop the commercial portions of Marina City were enough to make most people cringe and walk away. John's commitment to his vision is a testament to the power of specific intent and his willingness to take whatever steps were necessary to see it through to the end. That project and John's approach to making it happen are a prime example of a developer having the specific intent to prosper and the vision and commitment to follow through. That is why I chose a photograph of Marina City for the cover of this book. More about that later.

The point, for this book, is that if you want to accomplish something— anything of significance—you have to decide what it is you are going to do, then set out to do it. Obstacles will arise, but if you are absolutely clear in your mind that you are going to accomplish a specific objective and commit yourself to do what is necessary to accomplish that objective, you will more likely than not find a way to do it. The key is to decide, commit, and follow through.

This is as true for commercial real estate as it is for every other significant undertaking. It is true for specific projects, and it is true for pursuing a career in commercial real estate. If you are going to buy or develop commercial real estate or broker commercial real estate or be in the business of financing commercial real estate, or if you plan to become a commercial real estate attorney or a project manager for commercial real estate development or any of the many other commercial real estate roles you may wish to pursue, you must make a specific decision to follow that path, learn what you need to know to succeed, then take deliberate actions with the specific intent to make it happen.

To be clear, there are three distinct decisions to be made:

1. You must decide exactly what role you are going to play. Investor? Developer? Commercial real estate broker? Appraiser? Environmental consultant? Financial analyst? Loan underwriter? You name it. But decide what your role will be and write it down. By deciding and writing it down, you are making a commitment to yourself. You can later change your role if you decide otherwise, but the sooner you decide what your role will be, the sooner you will be on your way.

2. You must decide that you are going to undertake deliberate actions with the specific intent to prepare for and fulfill the role you have selected. *Deliberate actions* with *specific intent* are the key phrases.

3. Finally, you must begin. If you don't begin, you will never get beyond where you are today. It takes a huge amount of energy to

overcome inertia and start moving forward, but to move forward, you must begin. So begin. Begin. Begin. Begin. There is an ancient Chinese proverb, "A journey of a thousand miles begins with a single step." Begin. If you are discouraged that you should have started sooner, don't be. There is another Chinese proverb that states, "The best time to plant a tree was twenty years ago. The second best time is today." (Those ancient Chinese philosophers had a treasure trove of good ideas. Perhaps this is why China is the fastest-growing economic force in the world today.)

You don't need to know exactly how you are going to get where you are going. You just need to decide where you are going and then start taking deliberate actions to move yourself in the direction of where you have decided to go. As you act in a deliberate way to take you where you have decided to go, you will gain new information each step of the way, and the path will unfold before you.

This is true in every endeavor. If you live in Indiana and decide to climb a mountain in northern New Mexico, you might not know exactly the path you are going to take to the summit, but you do know that to get to the summit of that mountain, you at least need to get to New Mexico. If you are serious about climbing that mountain, get off your couch and head to New Mexico. It will not be coming to you.

Put yourself in a position to succeed. Find out what you need to succeed. Do you need a license? If you need a license, find out how to obtain that license and then do it. Is there certain information you need to succeed? Then find classes or books or a mentor that will teach you what you need to know and learn it.

There are many excellent sources of information to help you learn what you need to know. One I have found to be outstanding is the *CCIM Institute*. Its educational offerings include practical and insightful courses on all core topics essential for commercial real estate investment decision making. Check it out at the CCIM Web site: *www.ccim.com*. CCIM chapters exist in nearly every state and internationally in thirty-four countries outside the United States of America. Courses are taught throughout the year at numerous locations across the country. Many CCIM courses can be taken online. The depth of knowledge they impart is nothing short of remarkable. I highly recommend CCIM courses to anyone seriously interested in commercial real estate investment.

Valuable information and industry contacts can also be obtained by joining professional real estate organizations. Among my favorites in Chicago, Illinois, is the Chicago Real Estate Council (*http://chicagorec.org*).

Whatever you do, keep moving in the direction of your objective. Keep moving toward what you consider success. Begin, then keep moving, step by step by step in the direction of your objective until you get where you want to go.

If commercial real estate becomes your passion, there will be no end to your journey; save retirement or the end of your life. There is always another project to be developed and another investment opportunity to be seized. It's like playing Monopoly on a grand scale. New strategies. New challenges. New opportunities. You will never be bored.

# 5

# Vision Quest

Let's begin with this short exercise. Take out a piece of paper and a pen or pencil and answer the "vision quest" questions that follow. Spend about ten minutes, certainly no more than thirty. This is just to get you started.

1. What *exactly* do I intend to accomplish in the commercial real estate industry? In other words, what is my specific *vision* of the role I will play?

2. Is my *vision* big enough to dedicate a lifetime to living it and fulfilling it?

3. Have I started taking definite steps toward fulfilling my *vision*?

4. What specific steps have I taken in the past twelve months to move myself closer to fulfilling my *vision*?

5.  What specific steps will I take in the next twelve months to move me closer toward fulfilling my *vision*?

6.  What specific steps will I take this week?

7.  How will I know when I have begun to fulfill my *vision*?

8.  By what date do I intend to have concrete evidence that my *vision* is being fulfilled?

9.  How much time per week am I willing to commit to fulfilling my *vision*?

10. How much time will I spend this week pursuing my *vision*?

11. What is the first step I will take toward fulfilling my *vision*?

12. When will I begin?

# 6

# In Praise of Developers

Did I happen to mention I love real estate developers? Not like I love my wife or my kids or even my dog, but real estate developers are definitely among my favorite people.

Think about it.

Real estate developers are like gods. (Well, miniature gods, at least.) They create much of the physical world we inhabit. The homes and condominiums we live in. The grocery store and pharmacy down the street. The resorts and casinos and golf courses we enjoy for leisure. Restaurants. Shopping centers. Office buildings. Movie theaters. Truck terminals. Medical and surgical centers. Spas. Factories. Warehouses. Auditoriums. Parking garages. Hotels.

You name it; if it's *man-made*, attached to dirt, and we can get inside it, a real estate developer was probably involved.

Real estate developers are visionaries. They have the vision to recognize trends and the need for change. They recognize imbalances between what exists and what is needed. They see neighborhoods and towns and regions in flux as opportunities for renewal and improvement. Not only do real estate developers see opportunity, they seize it. They envision change and commit to it. Then work with it, massage it, shape it, squeeze it, stir it, shake it, blend it, juggle it, and make it happen.

How could anyone not love that?

Real estate developers are visionaries with a purpose. Visionaries who know how to transform their vision into reality. They are optimists. They are dreamers and doers wrapped into one. And for me, they are fun. Not funny necessarily, but fun to be around. Fun to work with. Fun to dream with.

I remember back in 1992 when John L. Marks of Mark IV Realty Group walked into my office and said he wanted to buy and redevelop the Marina City Commercial Complex in downtown Chicago. At the time, the Marina City Commercial Complex was a rathole. Largely vacant. In foreclosure. Languishing in bankruptcy. Burdened with nearly $10 million in unpaid and delinquent real estate taxes. Physically decaying and needing tens of millions of dollars in repairs. The residential condominium owners occupying the top forty floors of the two landmark corncob-shaped towers were understandably hostile and uncooperative, having been burned in the past by broken promises of prior owners.

Yet in all this mess, John saw opportunity. He had a vision that this dilapidated, decaying behemoth of an eyesore could be transformed into an economically viable and thriving jewel.

We spent most of the next four years working on that project. The transformation was remarkable. We had a blast making it happen.

Today, the Marina City Commercial Complex is home to the House of Blues, the unique and luxurious Hotel Sax, Smith & Wollensky Steak House, Bin 36 Wine Café, Crunch Fitness, 10pin Bowling Lounge, Marina Management, Skipper Bud's Marina, and numerous other thriving businesses. The pie-shaped condominiums starting above the twenty-story parking garage in each of the residential towers have risen substantially in value and offer some of the most dramatic skyline views in Chicago. The entire Marina City complex has been reestablished as a thriving mixed-use and entertainment mecca in the heart of Chicago.

Why? Because Chicago real estate developer John L. Marks had the vision and commitment to make it happen.

Did I mention I love real estate developers?

More recently, in the spring of 2005, I got the call to join the development team of Madkatstep Entertainment LLC.

Madkatstep Entertainment is a combined venture of Sears, Roebuck and Co., the retailing giant, and Ryan Companies US Inc., a remarkably creative and entrepreneurial real estate developer based in Minneapolis, Minnesota. (Yes, I love Ryan Companies too.)

It started with an idea.

Jeff Smith, Tim Gray, and Tim Hennelly of Ryan Companies US Inc. had the notion to build and own a sports and entertainment venue in an affluent community in need of convenient and unique entertainment options.

James Terrell, vice president of real estate at Sears Holdings Corporation, had the same notion. Sears, Roebuck and Co. had moved its corporate headquarters to Hoffman Estates, Illinois, in the early 1990s. As part of that move, Sears had acquired a large tract of adjacent land that was ready and available for development.

Hoffman Estates is a forward-looking community in a growing and affluent region northwest of Chicago in search of quality-of-life amenities for its residents. Its mayor, William D. McLeod, and its village manager, James H. Norris, saw the potential from the start.

It was a match made in heaven.

By the time I was called in as lead development counsel, Sears and Ryan had already negotiated a memorandum of understanding with the village of Hoffman Estates, setting forth a basic framework for the new Sears Centre Arena, including general terms for municipal financing.

A major tenant for the new Sears Centre Arena is a professional hockey team. A key development objective was to have the eleven-thousand-capacity, 240,000-square-foot arena built and ready for occupancy in time for the fall 2006 hockey season. It was already April 2005, only eighteen months from the target opening date. Even the most accelerated construction schedule required a minimum of fourteen months from groundbreaking to opening. Time was running out.

In the one-hundred-day rush that followed, the entire development team entered a zone and worked nearly around the clock with the village of Hoffman Estates.

The real estate developer, Ryan Companies US Inc., working closely with the real estate department at Sears, Roebuck and Co., negotiated agreements, confronted issues, overcame obstacles to obtain formal development approval, finalized municipal financing, formalized the naming rights agreement and ownership agreements, and accommodated project dissenters who were threatening litigation to delay or stop the arena from being built.

In the end, it was creativity, perseverance, and intense focus that led to the official groundbreaking for Sears Centre Arena on July 21, 2005. It is a unique sports and entertainment facility that will serve the village of

Hoffman Estates and neighboring towns for decades to come. It is already serving as an economic engine for complementary development that will provide new jobs, new opportunities, and a broadened tax base.

These two examples of creative development by visionary real estate developers are not unique. Between these two notable examples and beyond, the scenario plays out over and over in large and small development projects every day.

Renewal of functionally obsolete or declining shopping centers, warehouses, and other structures into modern and thriving enterprises.

Resurrection of blighted and decaying areas in cities and towns into homes and condominiums with retail and service businesses to support new neighborhoods.

Recycling of contaminated brownfields into safe and productive environments for consumers and business.

Greenfield developments to provide new opportunities, new jobs, and new services for emerging communities and families.

Real estate developers are seeing a need, stepping up to the challenge, and improving the world in which we live.

I have been blessed to work with some amazingly creative and dedicated real estate developers, both large and small, who are making a difference— and a profit—while having fun in the process.

Did I say fun? Maybe not during every moment while facing every challenge, but by and large, real estate developers are people who genuinely enjoy what they are doing. As a commercial real estate attorney, working with real estate developers has always been, for me, exhilarating.

Why do I love real estate developers? Ask yourself: How many times do you have the opportunity to work with people who make your job *exhilarating*? What's not to love about that?

So the next time you meet a real estate developer, please grab the developer's hand, look him or her directly in the eye, and say with deepest gratitude and sincerity,

*"Thank you! My friend Kymn Harp thinks you are the most wonderful person in the world. He loves you and thinks you are brilliant."* (Then slip him my business card or a copy of this book, and ask him to call me.)

*     *     *

By the way, so that you get my name right when you are talking to your developer friends, you may appreciate this assist:

My name *Kymn* is a family name and is pronounced "Kim." Think of Kymn as being like a *church hymn* with a *K* instead of an *H*. To remember this, associate my last name *Harp* with angels. Then if it helps, think of me as *Kymn Harp, the real estate developer's dirt angel* (with a law degree).

Thanks,<br>Kymn

# 7

# "It Ain't Rocket Science," but You *Do* Need to Know What You Are Doing!

| Albert Einstein: | *"Everything should be made as simple as possible, but not simpler."* |
|---|---|
| R. Kymn Harp: | $D^2 = I + F\eta$ |
| | *(Due diligence = Insight + Focused Investigation)* |

I'm a big fan of Albert Einstein. He's one of my intellectual heroes. He could see and understand what others could barely imagine. His greatest gift, I believe, was his ability to find answers to questions others didn't even know existed.

Real estate due diligence requires insight as well. To find the answers, you must know the questions.

Of course, I'm no Albert Einstein, but then, real estate due diligence is not intergalactic science.

The term itself is confusing. *Due diligence* is used grammatically like it's a thing or a process. "We need to complete our due diligence," or "Let me review your due diligence," or "Due diligence is expensive." I admit, I use it the same way.

In fact, however, *due diligence* is a standard of conduct. Due diligence refers to the degree of diligence we should exercise to investigate and analyze all important issues facing a particular transaction. That is to say, the degree of diligence that is *due* under the circumstances.

This definition has two important components:

1. a focus on *important issues* and
2. the degree of diligence appropriate under the circumstances of the particular transaction.

The art of the deal, so to speak, is in understanding what is *important* and what degree of investigation is due.

Failure to accurately identify these two threshold considerations will lead to one of two outcomes. The due diligence investigation will either be (1) incomplete, and therefore ineffective to discover and resolve the important transaction risks it is intended to protect against, or (2) overly broad, in which case it will be more time consuming and expensive than it needs to be. Either way, its value is diminished.

Due diligence can be expensive. We need to avoid making it more expensive than necessary.

So how do we make sure we get full value for our due diligence dollars? By making sure we know the right questions to ask and then answering them.

This requires two preliminary sets of questions:

First: What is the vision for this property? Why is it being acquired, and how will it be used?

Second: What is necessary to be known in order to confirm the vision can be fulfilled?

To be sure, we must know the first to answer the second. It is in answering the second that due diligence must be exercised.

For commercial real estate, there are four areas of concern:

1. Market demand
2. Access
3. Use
4. Finances

Once the vision is clear, addressing these four areas of concern will determine whether that vision can be fulfilled. Within these four areas of concern, we will find all the questions that need to be asked and answered to determine the feasibility of any commercial real estate transaction or project. How straightforward is that?

So what do these areas of concern entail? In simple terms, they can be summarized by a description of the inquiry they present.

# 1. Market Demand

*Market demand* asks this question: is the proposed project needed or wanted by target consumers in the geographic area within which the property is located?

Market demand is the most fundamental of the four aspects of commercial real estate. If there is no market demand, the transaction or project should not go forward. If you are developing, financing, or investing in a real estate project, make sure there is market demand for what is being offered. If you are a strategic owner intending to occupy and use the property yourself, market demand may be satisfied by your own business needs. If you are investing on speculation, be sure you know the demand of your intended market.

Determining market demand seldom involves a legal question. No attorney time is necessary. (See? I'm saving you money already.)

## 2. Access

*Access* asks this question: assuming adequate market demand to justify the proposed transaction or project, can target consumers seeking the goods or services to be offered at or from the property get to it with ease? This aspect includes evaluation of

a. existing or proposed highways, streets, and drives that will serve the site;
b. availability of in-and-out curb cuts for consumers and for delivery trucks and vans;
c. vehicular traffic flow to, from, and within the project site;
d. volume and convenience of pedestrian traffic;
e. ability of the project to accommodate the needs of the disabled in a manner compliant with Title III of the Americans with Disabilities Act (ADA), 42 USC Section 12181 et seq.;
f. adequacy of available parking (which, for business reasons, may need to be greater than the minimum required for zoning);
g. availability of public transportation; and
h. all other factors that may affect the flow of consumers and users to and from the site.

# 3. Use

*Use* asks this question: can the property be used as intended? This aspect includes an inquiry into

a. applicable zoning and private land use controls;
b. availability of utilities;
c. site topography;
d. quality of soil compaction to enable improvement using cost-effective methods of construction;
e. evaluation of the environmental condition of the property to determine whether environmental impediments exist that would prevent use of the property as intended absent remediation, institutional controls, or environmental impact mitigation; and
f. all other factors that may prevent the site from being used as intended.

# 4. Finances

*Finances* asks these questions: (a) Can funds be obtained to acquire, construct, and operate the project? And (b) will the investor receive an adequate return on investment to justify proceeding with the transaction or project?

To answer these questions, we must know the actual effective cost of acquisition or development and the net operating income and capital recovery expected to be generated by the project.

We must determine whether costly environmental remediation or institutional controls will be required, the amount of applicable user fees, environmental impact mitigation costs if any, real estate taxes, special assessments, tenant allowance or build-out requirements, and all other factors having an economic impact.

Although finances are primarily a business concern, certain aspects of project finance fall predominantly within the realm of legal due diligence.

~ Documentation of equity investments and project loans as well as hybrids, such as mezzanine financing, demand the attention of legal counsel.

~ If the property is leased, an evaluation of the amount, velocity and, durability of the revenue stream and any financial commitments of the owner/landlord are often considered by counsel.

~ Certainly, if public money is sought to reduce the net cost of development, legal counsel is required. We will discuss that in detail later in this book.

## Other Due Diligence Concerns

The four areas of concern described above pertain to the real estate aspects of the transaction. If you are dealing with commercial real estate, your due diligence must focus on these issues.

Every capital transaction has other due diligence concerns as well. These other concerns are beyond the scope of this chapter but may include issues pertaining to entity structure, authority of the parties, income and capital gains taxation and tax deferments, securities, and the overall structure of the transaction, to name just a few.

Commercial real estate due diligence is not rocket science, but it certainly helps if you know what you're looking for.

# 8

# Ten Things Every Buyer Needs to Close a Commercial Real Estate Loan

For thirty years, I have represented borrowers and lenders in commercial real estate transactions. During this time, it has become apparent that many buyers do not have a clear understanding of what is required to document a commercial real estate loan. Unless the basics are understood, the likelihood of success in closing a commercial real estate transaction is greatly reduced.

Throughout the process of negotiating the sale contract, all parties must keep their eye on what the buyer's lender will reasonably require as a condition to financing the purchase. This may not be what the parties want to focus on, but if this aspect of the transaction is ignored, the deal may not close at all.

Sellers and their agents often express the attitude that the buyer's financing is the buyer's problem, not theirs. Perhaps, but facilitating buyer's financing should certainly be of interest to sellers. How many sale transactions will close if the buyer cannot get financing?

This is not to suggest that sellers should intrude upon the relationship between the buyer and its lender or become actively involved in obtaining buyer's financing. It does mean, however, that the seller should understand what information concerning the property the buyer will need to produce to its lender to obtain financing, and that the seller should be prepared to fully cooperate with the buyer in all reasonable respects to produce that information.

## Basic Lending Criteria

Lenders actively involved in making loans secured by commercial real estate typically have the same or similar documentation requirements. Unless these requirements can be satisfied, the loan will not be funded. If the loan is not funded, the sale transaction will not likely close.

For nonpredatory lenders, the object, always, is to establish two basic lending criteria:

1. the ability of the borrower to repay the loan and
2. the ability of the lender to recover the full amount of the loan, including outstanding principal, accrued and unpaid interest, and all reasonable costs of collection, in the event the borrower fails to repay the loan.

In nearly every loan of every type, these two lending criteria form the basis of the lender's willingness to make the loan. Virtually all documentation in the loan closing process points to satisfying these two criteria. There are other legal requirements and regulations requiring lender compliance; but these two basic lending criteria represent, for the lender, what the loan closing process seeks to establish. They are also a primary focus of bank regulators, such as the FDIC, in verifying that the lender is following safe and sound lending practices.

Few lenders engaged in commercial real estate lending are interested in making loans without collateral sufficient to assure repayment of the entire loan even where the borrower's independent ability to repay is substantial.

As we have seen time and again, changes in economic conditions, whether occurring from ordinary economic cycles, changes in technology, natural disasters, divorce, death, or even terrorist attack or war, can change the *ability* of a borrower to pay. Prudent lending practices require adequate security for any loan of substance.

## Documenting the Loan

There is no magic to documenting a commercial real estate loan. There are issues to resolve and documents to draft, but all can be managed efficiently and effectively if all parties to the transaction recognize the legitimate needs of the lender and plan the transaction and the contract requirements with a view toward satisfying those needs within the framework of the sale transaction.

While the credit decision to issue a loan commitment focuses primarily on the ability of the borrower to repay the loan, the loan closing process focuses primarily on verification and documentation of the second-stated criteria: confirmation that the collateral is sufficient to assure repayment of the loan, including all principal, accrued and unpaid interest, late fees, attorney's fees, and other costs of collection, in the event the borrower fails to voluntarily repay the loan.

With this in mind, most commercial real estate lenders approach commercial real estate closings by viewing themselves as potential *backup buyers* and *immediate sellers*. They are always testing their collateral position against the possibility that the buyer/borrower will default, with the lender being forced to foreclose and become the owner of the property. Their documentation requirements are designed to place the lender, after foreclosure, in as good a position as they would require at closing if they were a sophisticated direct buyer of the property, with the expectation that the lender may need to promptly sell the property to a future sophisticated buyer to recover repayment of their loan.

# Top 10 Lender Deliveries

In documenting a commercial real estate loan, the parties must recognize that virtually all commercial real estate lenders will require, among other things, delivery of the following *property documents*:

1. operating statements for the past three years reflecting income and expenses of operations, including cost and timing of scheduled capital improvements;
2. certified copies of all leases;
3. A certified rent roll as of the date of the purchase contract and again as of a date within two or three days prior to closing;
4. estoppel certificates signed by each tenant (or typically tenants representing 90% of the leased GLA in the project) dated within fifteen days prior to closing;
5. Subordination, Nondisturbance, and Attornment Agreements (SNDA) signed by each tenant;
6. an ALTA lender's title insurance policy with required endorsements, including, among others, an ALTA 3.1 Zoning endorsement (modified to include parking), ALTA endorsement number 4 (contiguity endorsement insuring the mortgaged property constitutes a single parcel with no gaps or gores), and an access endorsement (insuring that the mortgaged property has access to public streets and ways for vehicular and pedestrian traffic);
7. copies of all documents of record which are to remain as encumbrances following closing, including all easements, restrictions, party wall agreements, and other similar items;
8. a current plat of survey prepared in accordance with 2005 minimum standard detail for ALTA/ACSM land title surveys certified to the lender, buyer, and the title insurer, including items 1 through 4, 6, 7(a), 7(b)(1), 8 through 11(a), and 14 from the surveyor's "Optional Survey Responsibilities and Specifications" referred to as *Table A*;

9. a satisfactory environmental site assessment (phase 1 audit) and, if appropriate under the circumstances, a subsurface environmental assessment (phase 2 audit) to demonstrate the property is not burdened with any recognized environmental condition; and

10. a site improvement's inspection report to evaluate the structural integrity of improvements.

To be sure, there will be other requirements and deliveries the buyer will be expected to satisfy as a condition to obtaining funding of the purchase money loan, but the items listed above are virtually universal. If the parties do not draft the purchase contract to accommodate timely delivery of these items to lender, the chances of closing the transaction are greatly reduced.

## Planning for Closing Costs

The closing process for commercial real estate transactions can be expensive. In addition to drafting the purchase contract to accommodate the documentary requirements of the buyer's lender, the buyer and his advisors need to consider and adequately plan for the high cost of bringing a commercial real estate transaction from contract to closing.

If competent buyer's counsel and competent lender's counsel work together, each understanding what is required to be done to get the transaction closed, the cost of closing can be kept to a minimum, though it will undoubtedly remain substantial. It is not unusual for closing costs for a commercial real estate transaction with even typical closing issues to run thousands of dollars. Buyers must understand this and be prepared to accept it as a cost of doing business.

Sophisticated buyers understand the costs involved in documenting and closing a commercial real estate transaction and factor them into the overall cost of the transaction just as they do costs such as the agreed upon purchase price, loan brokerage fees, loan commitment fees, and the like.

Closing costs can constitute significant transaction expenses and must be factored into the buyer's business decision-making process in determining whether to proceed with a commercial real estate transaction. They are inescapable expenditures that add to buyer's cost of acquiring commercial real estate. They must be taken into account to determine the "true purchase price" to be paid by the buyer to acquire any given project and to accurately calculate the anticipated yield on investment.

Some closing costs may be shifted to the seller through custom or effective contract negotiation, but many will unavoidably fall on the buyer. These can easily total tens of thousands of dollars in an even moderately sized commercial real estate transaction in the $1 million to $5 million price range.

Costs often overlooked, but ever present, include title insurance with required lender endorsements, an ALTA survey, environmental audit(s), a site improvements inspection report, and, somewhat surprisingly, buyer's attorney's fees.

For reasons that escape me, inexperienced buyers of commercial real estate, and even some experienced buyers, nearly always underestimate attorney's fees required in any given transaction. This is not because they are unpredictable since the combined fees a buyer must pay to its own attorney and to the lender's attorney typically aggregate around 1% of the purchase price. Perhaps it stems from wishful thinking associated with the customarily low attorney's fees charged by attorneys handling residential real estate closings. In reality, the level of sophistication and the amount of specialized work required to fully investigate and document a transaction for a buyer of commercial real estate make comparisons with residential real estate transactions inappropriate. Sophisticated commercial real estate investors understand this. Less sophisticated commercial real estate buyers must learn how to properly budget this cost.

Concluding negotiations for the sale/purchase of a substantial commercial real estate project is a thrilling experience, but until the transaction closes, it is only ink on paper. To get to closing, the contract must anticipate the documentation the buyer will be required to deliver to its lender to obtain purchase money financing. The buyer must also be aware of the substantial costs to be incurred in preparing for closing so that buyer may reasonably plan its cash requirements for closing. With a clear understanding of what is required and advanced planning to satisfy those requirements, the likelihood of successfully closing will be greatly enhanced.

# 9

# Commercial Real Estate Closing Costs: Who Pays What?

I am often asked how closing costs are typically divided between buyers and sellers in commercial real estate transactions.

Allocation of *closing costs* in a commercial real estate transaction is always subject to negotiation. Most allocations are decided by the parties as part of their contract negotiations. There are, however, certain general expectations and customary practices common throughout most of the United States. As a general proposition, the following cost allocations are likely to apply:

## *Seller Pays* for

1. Title policy with an extended coverage endorsement, but buyer pays for most other endorsements. In a minority of geographic areas, the buyer pays the full cost of title insurance. The justification given is that title insurance is for the benefit of the buyer in that it insures the buyer's title. The practical reality, however, is that title insurance is the means by which most sellers—especially sellers in urban areas—establish that they are conveying to buyer merchantable title.
2. A current ALTA survey, although if a seller has a fairly recent ALTA survey and the improvements on the parcel have not changed,

sellers often take the position that seller will provide the buyer and the title insurance company the survey seller has, with any update required to be obtained by buyer. Once again, this is a matter of negotiation.

3. UCC searches on any equipment or other personal property included in the sale (if applicable), although sellers sometimes assert this is part of the buyer's due diligence. As with title insurance, however, it is a means by which seller seeks to prove it is transferring clear title to the personal property seller is selling and is, therefore, commonly a seller charge.

4. State and county transfer taxes (in Illinois).

5. All property use expenses applicable to periods prior to closing.

6. Seller's title clearance expenses, such as the cost to pay off and release mortgages and other liens.

*Basically, the seller pays to establish that the seller owns what it is selling, and that the property it is selling is lien free.*

## *Buyer Pays* **for**

1. All environmental due diligence necessary to establish that buyer has conducted an *all appropriate inquiry* (discussed later, in chapter 22, titled "Turning Brownfields Green"). Sometimes, though not always or even usually, a purchase contract will provide for reimbursement to buyer for the cost of obtaining a phase 1 environmental site assessment and the cost of obtaining a phase 2 environmental site assessment, or either of them, if undisclosed environmental contamination is found that results in the transaction being terminated.

2. Geotechnical studies, such as subsurface environmental investigation, soil compaction studies, etc.

3. All title endorsements other than extended coverage, including especially any titled endorsements required for any lender's title insurance policy.

4. Municipal transfer taxes, unless provided otherwise by ordinance (in Illinois).
5. Special survey requirements, such as topographical contours, etc.
6. All property inspection expenses.
7. All property use expenses applicable from and after closing.
8. Buyer's financing expenses including, without limitation, costs of recording the mortgage and assignment of rents, etc., and also the cost of recording the deed.

*Basically, the buyer pays for all matters related to its due diligence investigation to verify that once buyer acquires and owns the property, the property can be used in a way that is satisfactory to buyer.* Buyer also pays for all expenses arising from loan requirements of its lender.

## Shared Expenses

These expenses are typically shared equally by the buyer and the seller:

1. Closing escrow (except buyer pays for its lender's escrow)
2. "New York-style" closing fee, if applicable

A "New York-style" closing refers to a closing that permits immediate disbursement of the sale proceeds upon delivery of the deed. In a "New York-style" closing, the title insurer assumes the risk of any adverse change in the condition of title during the *gap* period between the effective date of the most recent title examination and the date the deed is recorded. Title insurers charge an extra premium for taking the gap risk, which is commonly referred to as the "New York-style" closing fee. It is typically shared because both the buyer and the seller benefit. The buyer benefits because the closing is essentially completed upon delivery of the deed, enabling the buyer to immediately begin using the property as its own. The seller benefits because seller can immediately receive the sale proceeds, without the need to wait for recording of the deed and a later dated title search to cover the period from the effective date of the most recent title commitment to the date of recording.

As mentioned above, while this division is more or less customary, in any given transaction the actual negotiated allocation may be different.

# 10

# Keys to Closing Commercial Real Estate Transactions: Wading through the Mess

Anyone who thinks closing a commercial real estate transaction is a clean, easy, stress-free undertaking has never closed a commercial real estate transaction. Expect the unexpected, and be prepared to deal with it.

My father, Earl Harp, was a *land guy*. He assembled land, put in infrastructure, and sold it for a profit. His mantra: *"Buy by the acre, sell by the square foot."* From an early age, he drilled into my head the need to *"be a deal maker, not a deal breaker."* This was always coupled with the admonition *"If the deal doesn't close, no one is happy."* His theory was that attorneys sometimes *"kill tough deals"* simply because they don't want to be blamed if something goes wrong.

Over the years I learned that commercial real estate closings require much more than mere casual attention. Even a typically complex commercial real estate closing is a highly intense undertaking requiring disciplined and creative problem solving to adapt to ever-changing circumstances. In many cases, only focused and persistent attention to every detail will result in a successful closing. Commercial real estate closings are, in a word, *messy*.

A key point to understand is that commercial real estate closings do not *just happen*; they are made to happen. There is a time-proven method for successfully closing commercial real estate transactions. That method requires adherence to the four *keys to closing* outlined below:

# Keys to Closing

*1. Have a plan.* This sounds obvious, but it is remarkable how many times no specific plan for closing is developed. It is not a sufficient plan to merely say, "I like a particular piece of property; I want to own it." That is not a plan. That may be a goal, but that is not a plan.

A plan requires a clear and detailed vision of what, specifically, you want to accomplish and how you intend to accomplish it. For instance, if the objective is to acquire a large warehouse/light manufacturing facility with the intent to convert it to a mixed-use development with first-floor retail, a multideck parking garage, and upper-level condominiums or apartments, the transaction plan must include all the steps necessary to get from where you are today to where you need to be to fulfill your objective. If the intent, instead, is to demolish the building and build a strip shopping center, the plan will require a different approach. If the intent is to simply continue to use the facility for warehousing and light manufacturing, a plan is still required, but it may be substantially less complex.

In each case, developing the transaction plan should begin when the transaction is first conceived and should focus on the requirements for successfully closing upon conditions that will achieve the plan objective. The plan must guide contract negotiations so that the purchase agreement reflects the plan and the steps necessary for closing and postclosing use. If plan implementation requires particular zoning requirements or creation of easements or termination of party wall rights or confirmation of the structural integrity of building elements or availability of utilities or availability of municipal entitlements or environmental remediation and regulatory clearance or other identifiable requirements, the plan and the purchase agreement must address those issues and include those requirements as conditions to closing.

If it is unclear at the time of negotiating and entering into the purchase agreement whether all necessary conditions exist, the plan must include a suitable period to conduct a focused and diligent investigation of all issues material to fulfilling the plan. Not only must the plan include a period for investigation, the investigation must actually take place with all due diligence.

*Note*: The term is *due diligence*, not *do diligence*. The amount of diligence required in conducting the investigation is the amount of diligence required under the circumstances of the transaction to answer in the affirmative all questions that must be answered yes, and to answer in the negative all questions that must be answered no. The transaction plan will help focus attention on what these questions are. (See chapter 15, "Due Diligence: Checklists for Commercial Real Estate Transactions.")

2. *Assess and understand the issues.* Closely connected to the importance of having a plan is the importance of understanding all significant issues that may arise in implementing the plan. Some issues may represent obstacles, while others represent opportunities. One of the greatest causes of transaction failure is a lack of understanding of the issues or how to resolve them in a way that furthers the plan.

Various risk-shifting techniques are available and useful to address and mitigate transaction risks. Among them is the use of title insurance with appropriate use of available commercial endorsements. In addressing potential risk-shifting opportunities related to real estate title concerns, an understanding of the difference between a *real property law issue* and a *title insurance risk issue* is critical. Experienced commercial real estate counsel familiar with available commercial endorsements can often overcome what sometimes appear to be insurmountable title obstacles through creative draftsmanship and the assistance of a knowledgeable title underwriter.

Beyond title issues, there are numerous other transaction issues likely to arise as a commercial real estate transaction proceeds to closing. With commercial real estate, negotiations seldom end with execution of the purchase agreement.

New and unexpected issues often arise on the path toward closing that require creative problem solving and further negotiation. Sometimes these issues arise as a result of facts learned during the buyer's due diligence investigation. Other times they arise because independent third parties necessary to the transaction have interests adverse to, or at least different from, the interests of the seller, buyer, or buyer's lender. When obstacles arise, tailor-made solutions are often required to accommodate the needs of all concerned parties so the transaction can proceed to closing. To appropriately tailor a solution, you have to understand the issue and its impact on the legitimate needs of those affected.

3. *Recognize and overcome third-party inertia.* A major source of frustration, delay, and, sometimes, failure of commercial real estate transactions results from what I refer to as third-party inertia. Recognize that the closing deadlines important to transaction participants are often meaningless to unrelated third parties whose participation and cooperation is vital to moving the transaction forward. Chief among third-party dawdlers are governmental agencies, but the culprit may be any third-party vendor or other third party not controlled by the buyer or seller. For them, the transaction is often *just another file* on their already-cluttered desk.

Experienced commercial real estate counsel is often in the best position to recognize inordinate delay by third parties and can often cajole recalcitrant third parties into action with an appropriately timed telephone call. Often, experienced commercial real estate counsel will have developed relationships with necessary vendors and third parties through prior transactions and can use those established relationships to expedite the transaction at hand. Most importantly, however, experienced commercial real estate counsel is able to recognize when undue delay is occurring and push for a timely response when appropriate. Third-party vendors are human (they claim) and typically respond to timely appeals for action. It is the old cliché in action: "The squeaky wheel gets the oil." Care must be taken, however, to tactfully apply pressure only when necessary and appropriate. Repeated requests or demands for action when inappropriate to the circumstance run the risk of alienating a necessary party and adding to delay instead of eliminating it. Once again, human nature at work. Experienced commercial real estate counsel will often understand when to apply pressure and when to lay off.

4. *Prepare for the closing frenzy.* Like it or not, controlled chaos leading up to closing is the norm rather than the exception for commercial real estate transactions. It occurs because of the necessity of relying on independent third parties, the necessity of providing certifications and showings dated in close proximity to closing, and because new issues often arise at or near closing as a consequence of facts and information discovered through the continual exercise of due diligence on the path toward closing.

Whether dealing with third-party lessees, lenders, appraisers, local planning, zoning, or taxing authorities, public or quasi-public utilities, project surveyors, environmental consultants, title insurance companies, adjoining property owners, insurance companies, structural engineers, state or local departments of transportation, or other necessary third-party vendors or participants, it will often be the case that you must wait for them to react within their own time frame to enable the closing to proceed. The transaction is seldom as important to them as it is to the buyer and seller.

To the casual observer, building in additional lead time to allow for stragglers and dawdlers to act may seem to be an appropriate solution. The practical reality, however, is that many tasks must be completed within a narrow window of time just prior to closing.

As much as one may wish to eliminate the last-minute rush in the days just before closing, in many instances, it is just not possible. Many documents and *showings*, such as UCC searches, surveys, water department certifications, governmental notices, appraisals, property inspection reports, environmental site assessments, estoppel certificates, rent rolls, certificates of authority, and the like, must be dated near in time to the closing, often within a few days or weeks of closing. If prepared and dated too far in advance, they become stale and meaningless and must be redone, resulting in additional time and expense.

The reality is that commercial real estate closings often involve big dollar amounts and evolving circumstances. Rather than complain and stress out over the hectic pace of coordinating all closing requirements and conditions as closing approaches, you are wise to anticipate the fast-paced frenzy leading up to closing and should be prepared for it. As closing approaches, commercial real estate counsel, real estate brokers, and necessary representatives of the buyer and seller should remain available and ready to respond to changing demands and circumstances. This is not a time to go on vacation or to be on an out-of-town business trip. It is a time to remain focused and ready for action.

Recognizing that preclosing frenzy is the norm rather than an exception for commercial real estate transactions may help ease tension among the parties and their respective counsel and pave the way for a successful closing.

Like it or not, this is the way it is. Prepare for the frenzy and be available to respond. This is the way it works. Anyone who tells you differently is either lying to you or has had little experience in closing commercial real estate transactions.

\*　　\*　　\*

So there you have it. The four *keys to closing* a commercial real estate transaction.

1. Have a plan.
2. Assess and understand the issues.
3. Recognize and overcome third-party inertia.
4. Prepare for the closing frenzy.

Apply these keys to closing, and your chance of success goes up. Ignore these keys to closing, and your transaction may drift into oblivion.

# 11

# Uncommon View: Commercial Real Estate Development

A story I heard, growing up:

> When my grandfather was ten years old, he found a penny. With that penny, he bought a pencil. He sharpened that pencil then sold it for two cents. He took that two cents and bought two more pencils, sharpened them, and sold them for four cents. He reinvested his four cents in four more pencils, sharpened them, and sold them for eight cents. Then again, he bought eight more pencils, sharpened them, and sold them for sixteen cents. This went on until my grandfather had amassed $10.24. That's when my great-aunt Sophie died and left us her portfolio of shopping centers, office buildings, and rental homes. Our family has been in the real estate business ever since.

The story isn't true, but it taught four valuable lessons: (1) sweat equity is a powerful tool; (2) if you reinvest your earnings, wealth can grow geometrically; (3) the *big* money is in real estate; and (4) it would be nice to have a rich Aunt Sophie.

Like most families, we didn't have a rich Aunt Sophie, so my parents focused on lessons 1, 2, and 3.

I mention this story as a backdrop. My life growing up was always about real estate.

In my previous chapter, "Keys to Closing Commercial Real Estate Transactions," I mentioned my father because he was, and is, a wiz when it comes to commercial real estate. It was through him that I came to represent commercial real estate developers.

What I didn't mention was that my mother, Margaret Harp, was active in the family real estate business as well. While my father focused on commercial land development, my mother focused on residential real estate. I should have known better than to mention one but not the other. This chapter could be subtitled "Keys to Maintaining Harmony."

What does maintaining harmony have to do with commercial real estate development? Stick with me on this, then decide.

My mother cared about quality-of-life issues. Comfortable homes. Neighborhood parks. Safe streets. Good schools. Museums and other cultural enhancements.

I remember watching my mother lay out walking paths around detention ponds in residential developments and looking through catalogs, evaluating park benches and playground equipment for neighborhood parks. As a residential real estate investor, developer, and broker, my mother focused on *living environments*. If families were going to live in her neighborhoods, then the neighborhoods had to be *family friendly*.

As you might imagine, with my father focused on commercial development and my mother focused on residential quality-of-life issues, conversations around the dinner table were always interesting and sometimes dicey.

On one side of the table, my father envisioned expansive commercial development for retail shopping centers, office buildings, restaurants, hotels, theaters, warehouse superstores, entertainment centers, nightclubs, and more.

On the other side was my mother insisting upon neighborhoods with comfortable homes, safe streets, parks and other open areas, dry basements, clean air, clean water, and minimal noise and light pollution.

According to conventional wisdom—derived from public zoning board and plan commission hearings and community planning group meetings when commercial development is proposed near existing homes and neighborhoods—one might expect a clash of ideas turning into heated challenges and demands to forego development. Fortunately, our dinner table was nothing like most public hearings.

My mother and father each respected the vision of the other and understood the natural symbiotic relationship between residential and commercial development. Instead of complaining that one was trying to destroy the vision of the other, they anticipated each other's legitimate development and environmental needs and sought reasonable accommodation when possible. Sometimes they couldn't agree, but there was always a meaningful attempt to understand the viewpoint of the other, exchange ideas, and come to a mutually respectful and workable plan.

My mother was a resourceful advocate. She made my father think about how commercial development would affect residential neighbors and plan ways to mitigate adverse consequences on families. Long before coming into their current vogue, I learned at our family dinner table the concept of *lifestyle commercial centers* and complementary residential/commercial mixed-use developments.

The point for commercial developers and residential advocates is that they should each turn down the volume of their development debate and respectfully listen to what the other is saying. When the other has presented legitimate concerns or needs, those concerns and needs should be reasonably accommodated where possible. An idealistic dream? Perhaps. But I grew up watching it work.

To be sure, not all expressed concerns are legitimate, and not all proposed accommodations are possible. In those cases, resolution must necessarily be left up to public plan commissions, zoning boards, and municipal trustees or aldermen to arbitrate and decide the debate. As guardians of the public welfare entrusted with promoting the best interests of the community at large, they must decide. In a fair and evenhanded political environment, your best bet for prevailing is to demonstrate that you have listened with respect and have made reasonable and conscientious efforts to promote public harmony rather than discord.

*Point*: If you are a commercial real estate developer proposing a commercial development near existing residential neighborhoods, don't pretend they don't exist. Think about how they will be impacted, and include in your development plan ways to mitigate any adverse consequences created by your development. Talk to your residential neighbors. Listen to what they have to say. They are not *all* crazy. Sometimes (often, actually) they have legitimate concerns about real problems. If you can include in your development plan a way to economically fix a problem they already have (such as flooding, blight, inadequate parking, lack of sufficient parks or playgrounds, poor traffic circulation, etc.), your chances of favorable governmental action to approve your development plan goes up.

Whether you are a commercial real estate developer or a neighborhood advocate, understand that whether you like it or not, conditions change. Nothing stays the same. Obsolescence and blight are natural products of time. Redevelopment is coming. If not today, then someday.

*   *   *

Which brings me back to my point of promoting family harmony by making amends to my mother. You don't necessarily have to read what follows. This is primarily for her.

My mother retired a few years ago, but says she still enjoys reading my newsletters and articles. Perhaps a mother's love, but she always likes to read what I write about real estate and real estate development. She says her favorite is a poem I wrote about real estate development called "The Great Pyramids of Egypt Are in Disrepair." She thinks I should share it.

The poem was written in 1992. I have to admit, it never occurred to me that the poem was about *real estate development*. I can assure you, I was not consciously thinking about real estate development at the time I wrote it.

But my mother is a smart woman, and I have learned my lesson. I am not going to lightly cross her again. So in the interest of family harmony, here it is. I leave it to you to decide if it is about real estate development. If you don't think so, please don't tell my mother.

### The Great Pyramids of Egypt Are in Disrepair

We looked deep into each other's eyes and said:
"Our Love will last forever".

When I was two my parents built a new house
next door to the one we rented from my grandfather.
It was "ultra modern" with all the latest conveniences
A garbage disposer—dishwasher—central air—
central vac—wall-to-wall carpet—a private den—
We had a bird bath—and two hundred newly planted Scottish pines.

It's a parking lot now—
The church next door needed it.
Business was good.

The church doors were padlocked last year.
God moved down the street to nicer quarters.

I saw a news clip recently.
The Great Pyramids of Egypt are in disrepair.
They may not last unless work starts soon.
Sometimes the damage can be too great.
Even mummies get so wrapped up in what they are doing
they can begin to unravel.

Yesterday a friend asked: "Whatever happened to that girl?"

\*     \*     \*

The *point* (according to my mother):

Change happens.
What seems new and permanent today
Will be gone tomorrow.

No time stands still.
Real estate projects are no exception.
Redevelopment is coming.

# 12

# Perfect Seller!

Commercial real estate sellers are funny people. Not *ha-ha* funny, but funny in the sense that they sometimes have an odd way of looking at things.

This is not an indictment against any unique class of people. Let's face it, sooner or later, virtually all commercial real estate buyers become commercial real estate sellers. It is simply a recognition of an odd twist that occurs in the mind-set of many commercial real estate investors when the tables are turned and they become sellers instead of buyers.

Generally, once a seller has made the decision to *sell*, most sellers want to move ahead with as little pain and delay as possible. Right?

What typically happens? The seller finds a commercial real estate broker and lists the property. Once the seller receives a letter of intent or contract offer, the seller contacts its attorney to prepare or review the contract. The contract is virtually always subject to a *due diligence review* period during which the buyer is to investigate the property to determine whether it satisfies buyer's use or investment criteria. The contract invariably includes a variety of *seller deliveries*: a title commitment, copies of documents of record, ALTA survey, a rent roll, copies of leases, service contracts, etc.

So what does the typical seller do?

Often the seller waits until the contract is fully executed before ordering title, obtaining copies of documents of record, compiling leases, ordering a survey, and gathering other required seller deliveries.

Worse, many sellers adopt the attitude that "buyer's financing and due diligence are buyer's problem—leave me out of it."

While it is certainly true that buyer's financing and due diligence are the responsibility of the buyer, it is also true that much of the information a buyer needs must be obtained from the seller. If the buyer is delayed or obstructed in obtaining necessary information, it will be delayed in performing its due diligence review and unable to satisfy necessary conditions for financing. Even if the contract is "not contingent on financing," the practical reality—in most cases—is that if financing is not obtained, the transaction will not close. Failure to take reasonable steps to facilitate buyer's due diligence and financing, then, ultimately becomes the *seller's problem*.

What *should* a seller do?

Sellers should become proactive instead of reactive.

Instead of waiting until a letter of intent is received or a contract is signed before compiling information a buyer will almost certainly need, a seller should compile the information a buyer will need as soon as the seller decides to sell.

How does a seller know what the buyer will need? Interesting question. When the seller was a buyer, he/she knew exactly what a buyer needed to evaluate the property, get financing, and close. Still, even if amnesia has set in, what a buyer needs is fairly predictable. (See chapter 8, "Ten Things Every Buyer Needs to Close a Commercial Real Estate Loan.")

If you are a seller and are indeed committed to selling your property, sooner or later, you are going to be called upon to deliver at least the typical seller deliveries. Sooner is better than later. It will speed up the due diligence process and enable the buyer to determine at the earliest possible date whether there are obstacles to closing.

Once gathered, the seller deliveries should be bound in a *due diligence binder* for distribution to interested buyers.

It will typically expedite the transaction if the due diligence binder is delivered to the buyer when the buyer is first seriously considering purchase of a property—even before the purchase contract is drafted. If, in fact, conditions do exist that prevent a buyer from proceeding to closing, it is in seller's interest to find out now rather than later so the property can be kept on the market and made available to a buyer who may be in a position to proceed.

Certainly, a seller may require a prospective buyer to sign a confidentiality, nonuse, and nondisclosure agreement as a condition to receiving the due diligence binder if the seller feels this is desirable.

If the documents are voluminous (such as if the property is a large shopping center, office building, or mixed-use development with many tenants), an alternative is to establish a so-called war room where copies of all the documents are maintained and can be made readily available for inspection by prospective buyers. Even then, all title-related documents should be compiled in a due diligence binder or CD-ROM for ready access and review by the buyer's attorney.

What should the due diligence binder or war room include? At a minimum, it should include the following:

1. Current commitment for title insurance

2. Copies of all documents of record referred to in the commitment for title insurance which will remain on schedule B of the commitment of title insurance after closing (i.e., easements, restrictions, covenants, etc.)

3. Current real estate tax bill(s)

4. A current ALTA survey showing all improvements as currently exist, ideally including items 1 through 4, 6, 7(a), 7(b)(1), 8 through 11(a) and 14 from table A of the (2005) optional survey requirements for ALTA surveys

5. If the property is income producing, operating statements for the past three years, a current rent roll, and copies of all leases, licenses, and concessions (don't forget about cell-tower leases and billboard or sign leases and parking leases)

6. A schedule of any personal property to be included

7. If the property is an out lot or otherwise part of a larger whole and is required to participate in payment of common area maintenance (CAM) charges, copies of invoices and CAM charge breakdowns for at least the past two years

8. Service contracts (for elevator, fire/sprinkler maintenance, scavenger, snow removal and landscaping, security, etc.)

9. Any available environmental site assessment reports (phase 1 and phase 2) and, certainly, any NFR letters or governmental notices relating to environmental issues

10. All existing blueprints, building plans, site plans, schematics, soil compaction test reports, structural reports, roof warranties, and other information relating to existing improvements

To the extent practical, a seller should compile all information in its possession or control that a seller would reasonably want to see if it were a buyer conducting its own due diligence review to decide whether to purchase the property. Refer to chapter 15, "Due Diligence Checklists for Commercial Real Estate Transactions."

If you are a *really* bold seller, you might even consider preparing and including with the due diligence binder a bare-boned but workable form of purchase agreement you would be willing to accept if tendered with an acceptable purchase price from a qualified buyer.

Of course, to be a *perfect seller*, you need to understand the issues presented by the due diligence binder's contents, especially as they relate to access, use and finances, and be prepared to work with the buyer to resolve problematic issues to get the transaction to closing.

## *Seller Resistance*

Sellers are sometimes reluctant to voluntarily offer this information up front. Why? There are four common reasons.

1. Some sellers think they should not volunteer anything. That maybe the buyer will forget to ask for that *one document* that reveals a defect, thereby enabling the seller to *get away with* selling the property without addressing the issue.

If this is the thinking, it is naïve and shortsighted. What is more likely to happen is that the buyer will discover the defect during its due diligence investigation and will either terminate the transaction or demand a significant price concession under the threat of contract termination.

On the other hand, it has been my experience that if the defect is disclosed at the outset, when the buyer is enthusiastically formulating the project concept, resolution of the issue may be factored into the buyer's development plan and never again become a major transaction issue.

2. Another reason I hear is that the seller does not wish to prematurely incur the expense of pulling the due diligence materials together *in*

*case transaction falls apart.* The seller is concerned with *wasting money.*

My response to this is twofold: (i) If the seller is committed to selling the property, the expenditure is not wasted even if the current transaction fails because most of the information will be useful when the next buyer comes along, and (ii) the benefit of facilitating buyer's due diligence and accelerating closing will often far exceed the carrying cost of compiling this information in advance. Besides, the sooner you can get to closing, the more likely the transaction is to close.

3.  A variation of the *money* theme is the notion that once a buyer spends large amounts of money performing due diligence, the buyer becomes committed to the deal and is more likely to close. This may occasionally be true, but experience shows that most buyers will walk away rather than throw good money away chasing a bad deal. The result is that the property may then need to go back on the market to start from square one. If this happens more than once, the property may gain a reputation as a *problem property*, thereby depressing its value in the marketplace.

4.  The best reason I hear (usually from other lawyers) is that volunteering this information risks exposing the seller to liability on a theory of seller implicitly warranting the accuracy and all-inclusiveness of the contents of the due diligence binder.

My response is that it takes only a little bit of creative draftsmanship to mitigate this risk. Further, preparing and offering a well-constructed due diligence binder documents seller's deliveries and positions the seller to avoid most contractual and implied warranties, thereby reducing a seller's exposure to liability.

## *What Are the Advantages to a Seller?*

If you are a seller of commercial or industrial real estate and conscientiously follow the recommendations outlined above, your transaction will proceed more smoothly and quickly, the likelihood of closing will increase, and you will save money by avoiding the need to renegotiate issues that should have been addressed at the outset of the transaction.

To be sure, other issues will arise. They always do. But your chances of proceeding to closing on time and on budget will greatly increase if you make the effort to be as close to a perfect seller as possible.

\* \* \*

*Note to brokers*: If you are a commercial real estate broker, I encourage you to discuss with your seller the strategy outlined in this chapter the moment the property is listed for sale. Give them a copy of this book with a one-hundred-dollar bill as a bookmark at the beginning of this chapter. Recommend that they read it. I assure you, if your seller follows the advice in this chapter, everyone will benefit.

# 13

# Lending Blind:
# What You Don't Know Can Hurt You

What is *lending blind*? *Lending blind* is approaching commercial real estate lending with substantially the same approach as lending to residential homeowners. Lending blind is making loans secured by commercial real estate without fully understanding the underlying commercial real estate project and the collateral risks it presents. Lending blind is closing one's eyes to important legal, environmental, and land use issues uniquely applicable to commercial real estate and ignoring available risk-shifting techniques in the hope or unfounded belief that if the issues are not carefully considered, maybe they won't exist.

Make no mistake: Commercial real estate lending is not the same as residential real estate lending. Many bankers and other lenders faced with customer resistance to higher loan costs may wish to close their eyes to this reality. Ignoring this reality, however, does not change it. Ignoring this reality may on the surface seem to cut costs, but it can endanger bank profits and jeopardize capital.

*Sound and safe lending practices* is not just a phrase used by banking regulators. It should be a way of doing business.

Failing to focus on genuine risks presented by commercial real estate lending is not a sound and safe lending practice.

Believing a commercial real estate loan is properly documented through use of prepackaged computer-generated loan documents, without also requiring qualified, in-depth analysis of land-use controls imposed by documents of record and zoning, knowledgeable examination of survey, lease subordination, title insurance, access, borrower authority and other legal issues, and without fully understanding environmental risks presented by existing, former, or contemplated tenants, occupiers, and adjacent landowners, is not following sound and safe lending practices.

Blindly following a loan document checklist and filling the loan file with documents and materials that *evidence* a well-documented loan, without a genuine understanding of the limitations, pitfalls, and legal red flags the documents may raise, is not following sound and safe lending practices.

Using the ostrich approach to lending is like a game of Russian roulette. You might get away with it for a while, but the result can be catastrophic to bank profits and capital if and when the loan goes bad.

Banks and other commercial lenders following these unsound and unsafe banking practices do not like this message. They often assert their loan processors are *good people* with excellent training and years of experience using their canned document software.

The fact that a lender's in-house loan processors are *good people* is not in question. The fact that they are well trained to input relevant data so a computer can generate a beautiful set of loan documents is not the issue.

The issue is what may lie beyond the documents.

A perfectly generated set of *standard loan documents* may be of little value if they fail to adequately address unique issues raised by the commercial real estate project serving as collateral. To be certain, each commercial real estate project is different. Unlike owner-occupied residential real estate, it

63

cannot safely be *assumed* that commercial real estate collateral is legally suitable for, or can even legally be used for, its intended use.

A beautifully drafted mortgage on commercial real estate is of little value if the project does not have a legal right to commercially reasonable access or parking. *Case in point*: how secure is a loan on an eight-hundred-person banquet facility in a mixed-use center if the banquet facility has a legal right to park only 155 cars? *Case in point*: what is the collateral value of a hotel on a highly visible highway interchange, which has as its primary means of access only a license to use a private drive that can be closed at any time? (Is the appraiser legally responsible for discovering this fact when making the loan appraisal? What kind of access does the typical title insurance policy insure?)

Obtaining a lender's title insurance policy with specialized commercial endorsements is a useful method of shifting risks away from the lender, but the lender must understand how to interpret each endorsement to know what it insures. *Case in point*: While attending a loan closing as an *accommodation* for a lender making a large loan to one of its *best customers* to purchase a warehouse and manufacturing building, with instructions from the lender to simply *oversee execution of closing documents (the lender had prepared) and approve title*, it was discovered by lender's counsel upon review of the lender's required zoning endorsement that the borrower's intended use of the facility was expressly prohibited by the applicable zoning ordinance. The ALTA 3.1 Zoning endorsement to be attached to the loan policy disclosed that the borrower's intended use was expressly excluded as a permitted use on the land. Neither the lender nor the borrower had read the endorsement, or if they had, they failed to understand its meaning. The transaction was aborted by the regretful but thankful borrower, who would have been unable to operate its business if the transaction had proceeded. Failure to recognize this restriction before funding would have almost certainly meant bankruptcy for one of the bank's *best customers* and a huge nonperforming loan for the lender.

Experience shows that lenders should not assume that borrowers and their counsel will always conduct an adequate due diligence investigation to ascertain all associated risks that may impact the project and important underlying assumptions for a loan.

A lender must also avoid the trap of overreliance upon a borrower's representations and warranties in the loan documents. If the borrower is mistaken, what is the consequence? Declaring a material default? *Case in point*: A mortgage securing a $1.65 million loan contained a warranty from borrower that *all leases encumbering the real estate are, and shall remain, subordinate to the lien of the mortgage.* One lease was, in fact, not automatically subordinate to the mortgage. The lender's title insurance policy included an exception for all existing leases and tenancies. The nonsubordinated lease contained a lessee's option to purchase the entire strip center for $1.52 million. Will declaring a default for breach of warranty solve this defect? What is the lender's collateral position if the lessee exercises its option to purchase?

The business of lending is about making sound and safe loans that profitably perform as planned. Yield is the key. Not foreclosure. The ability to declare a default and start enforcement and foreclosure proceedings is a remedy of last resort. It is not a viable substitute for diligent evaluation of material loan predicates and will rarely fix problems with underlying collateral.

Sound and safe lending requires comprehensive understanding of all relevant issues confronting each commercial real estate project serving as collateral. If lenders are going to make commercial real estate loans, they should be following sound and safe lending practices. To do this, they must either learn how to fully and meaningfully evaluate all the attendant risks associated with their collateral or engage counsel with specialized knowledge and experience in commercial real estate lending to perform this function.

Turning a blind eye to the uniqueness of commercial real estate collateral and to the limitations of many well-meaning but unknowing in-house loan processors is neither a sound nor a safe lending practice.

Independent, focused, and knowledgeable lender due diligence is a must.

**14**

# Commercial Real Estate Transaction
# *Due Diligence*—What Is It?

Due diligence is generally referred to as a *process*. It is actually a standard of conduct for conducting the process of investigating and discovering all material facts and information important to the project at hand. The term *due diligence* is used as shorthand for the process of answering in the affirmative all questions that must be answered yes and answering in the negative all questions that must be answered no. It is the research, discovery, or confirmation of all that is necessary to make a commercial real estate project or transaction a success, using all diligence due under the circumstances.

Note that the term is *due diligence, not* "do" diligence. It is the exercise of such degree of diligence appropriate to the circumstance. Not every avenue of inquiry is relevant to every transaction.

The *secret* to cost-effective due diligence is tailoring the inquiry to the specific objectives of the party for whom the investigation is being conducted.

To be effective, due diligence must be exercised from the initial contemplation of a project through its conclusion and beyond. It never really ends. Unfortunately, for some, it never really begins.

# 15

# Due Diligence Checklists for Commercial Real Estate Transactions

Are you planning to purchase, finance, or develop any of the following types of commercial or industrial real estate?

- Shopping center
- Office building
- Restaurant/banquet property
- Parking lot/parking garage
- Retail store
- Gas station
- Manufacturing facility
- Distribution center
- Logistics terminal
- Medical building
- Nursing home
- Hotel/motel
- Mixed use
- Pharmacy
- Special use facility
- Other

A *key* element to successfully investing in commercial or industrial real estate is performing an adequate due diligence investigation prior to becoming legally bound to acquire the property. An adequate due diligence investigation will assure awareness of all material facts relevant to the intended use or disposition of the property after closing.

The following checklists will help you conduct a focused and meaningful due diligence investigation.

## *Basic Due Diligence Concepts*

*Caveat emptor:* Let the buyer beware.

Consumer protection laws applicable to home purchases seldom apply to commercial real estate transactions. The rule that a buyer must examine, judge, and test for himself applies to the purchase of commercial real estate.

*Due Diligence:* "Such a measure of prudence, activity, or assiduity, as is proper to be expected from, and ordinarily exercised by, a reasonable and prudent [person] under the particular circumstances; not measured by any absolute standard, but depending upon the relative facts of the special case" (*Black's Law Dictionary* [West Publishing Company]).

Contractual representations and warranties are *not* a substitute for due diligence. Breach of representations and warranties = Litigation, time, and expense.

The point of commercial real estate due diligence is to avoid transaction surprises and confirm the property can be used as intended.

* * *

# What Diligence Is Due?

The scope, intensity, and focus of any due diligence investigation of commercial or industrial real estate depend upon the objectives of the party for whom the investigation is conducted. These objectives may vary depending upon whether the investigation is conducted for the benefit of (i) a strategic buyer (or long-term lessee), (ii) a financial buyer, (iii) a developer, or (iv) a lender.

If you are a seller, understand that to close the transaction your buyer and its lender must address all issues material to their respective objectives—some of which require information only you, as owner, can adequately provide.

## General Objectives

i.   A *strategic buyer* (or long-term lessee) is acquiring the property for its own use and must verify that the property is suitable for that intended use.

ii.  A *financial buyer* is acquiring the property for the expected return on investment generated by the property's anticipated revenue stream and must determine the amount, velocity, and durability of the revenue stream. A sophisticated financial buyer will likely calculate its yield based upon discounted cash flows rather than the much less precise capitalization rate (cap rate) and will need adequate financial information to do so.

iii. A *developer* is seeking to add value by changing the character or use of the property—usually with a short-term to intermediate-term exit strategy to dispose of the property, although a developer might plan to hold the property long term as a financial buyer after development or redevelopment. The developer must focus on whether the planned change in character or use can be accomplished in a cost-effective manner.

iv.  A *lender* is seeking to establish two basic lending criteria:

1. *Ability to repay*—the ability of the property to generate sufficient revenue to repay the loan on a timely basis, *and*

2. *Sufficiency of collateral*—the objective disposal value of the collateral in the event of a loan default to assure adequate funds to repay the loan, carrying costs, and costs of collection in the event forced collection becomes necessary.

The amount of diligent inquiry due to be expended (i.e., *due diligence*) to investigate any particular commercial or industrial real estate project is the amount of inquiry required to answer each of the following questions to the extent relevant to the objectives of the party conducting the investigation:

# I.   The Property

1. Exactly what *property* does the purchaser believe it is acquiring?
   - Land
   - Building
   - Fixtures
   - Other improvements
   - Other rights
   - The entire fee title interest including all air rights and subterranean rights
   - All development rights

2. What is purchaser's planned use of the property?

3. Does the physical condition of the property permit use as planned?
   - Commercially adequate access to public streets and ways
   - Sufficient parking

- Structural condition of improvements
- Environmental contamination
    o Innocent purchaser defense versus exemption from liability
    o All appropriate inquiry

4. Is there any legal restriction to purchaser's use of the property as planned?
   - Zoning
   - Private land use controls
   - Americans with Disabilities Act
   - Availability of licenses
   - Liquor license
   - Entertainment license
   - Outdoor dining license
   - Drive-through windows permitted
   - Other impediments

5. How much does purchaser expect to pay for the property?

6. Is there any condition on or within the property that is likely to increase purchaser's effective cost to acquire or use the property?
   - Property owner's assessments
   - Real estate tax in line with value
   - Special assessment
   - Required user fees for necessary amenities
     - Drainage
     - Access
     - Parking
     - Other

7. Any encroachments onto the property or from the property onto other lands?

8. Are there any encumbrances on the property that will not be cleared at closing?
   - Easements
   - Covenants running with the land
   - Liens or other financial servitudes
   - Leases

9. If the property is subject to any leases, are there any
   - security deposits,
   - options to extend term,
   - options to purchase,
   - rights of first refusal,
   - rights of first offer,
   - maintenance obligations,
   - duty of landlord to provide utilities,
   - real estate tax or CAM escrows,
   - delinquent rent,
   - prepaid rent,
   - tenant mix controls,
   - tenant exclusives,
   - tenant parking requirements,
   - automatic subordination of lease to future mortgages,
   - other material lease terms?

10. New construction?
    - Availability of construction permits
    - Soil conditions
    - Utilities
    - NPDES (National Pollutant Discharge Elimination System) permit
      o Phase 2 effective March 2003—permit required if earth is disturbed on one acre or more of land

      o   If applicable, Stormwater Pollution Prevention Plan (SWPPP) is required.

## II. The Seller

1. Who is the seller?
   - Individual
   - Trust
   - Partnership
   - Corporation
   - Limited liability company
   - Other legally existing entity

2. If other than natural person, does the seller validly exist and is the seller in good standing?

3. Does the seller own the property?

4. Does the seller have authority to convey the property?
   - Board of director approvals
   - Shareholder or member approval
   - Other consents
   - If foreign individual or entity, are there any special requirements applicable?
     - o   Qualification to do business in jurisdiction of property
     - o   Federal Tax Withholding
     - o   U.S. Patriot Act compliance

5. Who has authority to bind the seller?

6. Are sale proceeds sufficient to pay off all liens?

# III. The Purchaser

1. Who is the purchaser?

2. What is the purchaser/grantee's exact legal name?

3. If the purchaser/grantee is an entity, has it been validly created, and is it in good standing?

   - Articles of incorporation or articles of organization
   - Certificate of good standing

4. Is the purchaser/grantee authorized to own and operate the property and, if applicable, finance acquisition of the property?
   - Board of director approvals
   - Shareholder or member approval
   - If foreign individual or entity, are any special requirements applicable?
     o Qualification to do business in jurisdiction of the property
     o U.S. Patriot Act compliance
     o Bank Secrecy Act/Anti-Money Laundering compliance

5. Who is authorized to bind the purchaser/grantee?

# IV. Purchaser Financing

### A. Business Terms of the Loan

1. What loan terms have the borrower and its lender agreed to?
   - What is the amount of the loan?
   - What is the interest rate?

- What are the repayment terms?
- What is the collateral?
  - o Commercial real estate only
  - o Real estate and personal property together
  - o First lien
  - o A junior lien
- Is it a single advance loan?
- A multiple advance loan?
- A construction loan?
- If it is a multiple advance loan, can the principal be reborrowed once repaid prior to maturity of the loan, making it, in effect, a revolving line of credit?
- Are there reserve requirements?
  - o Interest reserves
  - o Repair reserves
  - o Real estate tax reserves
  - o Insurance reserves
  - o Environmental remediation reserves
  - o Other reserves

2. Are there requirements for the borrower to open business operating accounts with the lender? If so, is the borrower obligated to maintain minimum compensating balances?

3. Is the borrower required to pledge business accounts as additional collateral?

4. Are there early repayment fees or yield maintenance requirements (each sometimes referred to as prepayment penalties)?

5. Are there repayment blackout periods during which the borrower is not permitted to repay the loan?

6. Is a profit participation payment to the lender required upon disposition?

7. Is there a loan commitment fee or *good faith deposit* due upon borrower's acceptance of the loan commitment?

8. Is there a loan funding fee or loan brokerage fee or other loan fee due the lender or a loan broker at closing?

9. What are the borrower's expense reimbursement obligations to the lender? When are they due? What is the borrower's obligation to pay the lender's expenses if the loan does not close?

**B. Documenting the Commercial Real Estate Loan**

Does the purchaser have all information necessary to comply with the lender's loan closing requirements?

Not all loan documentation requirements may be known at the outset of a transaction, although most commercial real estate loan documentation requirements are fairly typical. Some required information can be obtained only from the seller. Production of that information to the purchaser for delivery to its lender must be required in the purchase contract.

As guidance to what a commercial real estate lender may require, the following sets forth a typical closing checklist for a loan secured by commercial real estate.

## Commercial Real Estate Loan Closing Checklist

1. Promissory note

2. Personal guaranties (which may be full, partial, secured, unsecured; payment guaranties; collection guaranties; or a variety of other types of guarantees as may be required by lender)

3. Loan agreement (often incorporated into the promissory note and/or mortgage in lieu of being a separate document)

4. Mortgage (sometimes expanded to be a mortgage, security agreement, and fixture filing)

5. Assignment of rents and leases

6. Security agreement

7. Financing statement (sometimes referred to as a UCC-1 or Initial Filing)

8. Evidence of borrower's existence in good standing, including

    a. Certified copy of organizational documents of borrowing entity (including Articles of Incorporation if the borrower is a corporation, Articles of Organization or Certificate of Formation, and written operating agreement if the borrower is a limited liability company, certified copy of trust agreement with all amendments if the borrower is a land trust or other trust, etc.)

    b. Certificate of Good Standing (if a corporation or LLC) or Certificate of Existence (if a limited partnership) or Certificate of Qualification to Transact Business (if the borrower is an entity doing business in a state other than its state of formation)

9. Evidence of borrower's authority to borrow, including

    a. Borrower's Certificate

    b. Certified Resolutions

    c. Incumbency Certificate

10. Satisfactory commitment for title insurance (which will typically require, for analysis by the lender, copies of all documents of

record appearing on schedule B of the title commitment, which are to remain after closing), with required commercial title insurance endorsements, often including

a. Affirmative creditors' rights endorsement (extending coverage over policy exclusion 7 and policy exclusions 3[a] and 3[d] as they relate to creditor's rights matters)

b. ALTA 3.1 Zoning endorsement modified to include parking (although if the property is a multiuser property, such as a retail shopping center, an ALTA 3.0 Zoning endorsement may be appropriate)

c. ALTA comprehensive endorsement 1

d. Location endorsement (street address)

e. Access endorsement (vehicular access to public streets and ways)

f. Contiguity endorsement (the insured land comprises a single parcel with no gaps or gores)

g. PIN endorsement (insuring that the identified real estate tax permanent index numbers are the only applicable PIN numbers affecting the collateral and that they relate solely to the real property comprising the collateral)

h. Usury endorsement (insuring that the loan does not violate any prohibitions against excessive interest charges)

i. Other title insurance endorsements applicable to protect the intended use and value of the collateral, as may be determined upon review of the commitment for title insurance and survey or arising from the existence of special issues pertaining to the transaction or the borrower

11. Current ALTA/ACSM land title survey (three sets), prepared in accordance with the 2005 Minimum Standard Detail Requirements for ALTA/ACSM Land Title Surveys including items 1 through 4, 6, 7(a), 7(b)(1), 8 through 11(a), and 14 from Table A: Optional

Survey Responsibilities and Specifications (generally referred to simply as Table A)

12. Current rent roll
13. Certified copy of all leases (four sets—one each for the buyer, buyer's attorney, title company, and the lender)
14. Lessee estoppel certificates
15. Lessee Subordination, Nondisturbance, and Attornment Agreements (sometimes referred to simply as SNDAs)
16. UCC, judgment, pending litigation, bankruptcy, and tax lien search report
17. Appraisal—complying with Title XI of FIRREA (Financial Institutions Reform, Recovery and Enforcement Act of 1989, as amended)
18. Environmental Site Assessment report (sometimes referred to as Environmental Phase I and/or Phase 2 Audit reports)
19. Environmental Indemnity Agreement (signed by the borrower and guarantors)
20. Site improvements inspection report
21. Evidence of hazard insurance naming the lender as the mortgagee/lender loss payee and liability insurance naming the lender as an *additional insured* (sometimes listed as simply Acord 27 and Acord 25 respectively)
22. Legal opinion of borrower's attorney
23. Credit underwriting documents, such as signed tax returns, property operating statements, etc., as may be specified by the lender
24. Compliance Agreement (sometimes also called an Errors and Omissions Agreement) whereby the borrower agrees to correct, after closing, errors or omissions in loan documentation

\*     \*     \*

It is useful to become familiar with the lender's loan documentation requirements as early in the transaction as practical. The requirements will likely be set forth with some detail in the lender's loan commitment, which is typically much more detailed than most loan commitments issued in residential transactions.

Conducting the due diligence investigation in a commercial real estate transaction can be time-consuming and expensive in all events.

If the loan requirements cannot be satisfied, it is better to make that determination during the contractual *due diligence period*—which typically provides for a so-called *free out*—rather than at a later date when the earnest money may be at risk of forfeiture or when other liability for failure to close may attach.

\* \* \*

Conducting an effective due diligence investigation in a commercial or industrial real estate transaction to discover all material facts and conditions affecting the property and the transaction is of critical importance.

Unlike owner-occupied residential real estate, when a house can nearly always be occupied as the purchaser's home, commercial and industrial real estate acquired for business use or for investment is impacted by numerous factors that may limit its use and value.

The existence of these factors and their impact on a purchaser's ability to use the property as intended can only be discovered through diligent and focused investigation and attention to detail.

Exercise due diligence.

# 16

# Pop Quiz!

I read once that if you took all the real estate lawyers in North America and laid them end to end along the equator, it would be a good idea to leave them there.

That's what I read.

What do you suppose that means?

I cannot overemphasize the need to exercise due diligence when purchasing commercial real estate. The need to investigate, before closing, every significant aspect of the property you are acquiring. The importance of evaluating each commercial real estate transaction with a mind-set that once the closing occurs, there is no going back. The seller has your money and is gone. If postclosing problems arise, the seller's contract representations and warranties will, at best, mean expensive litigation. Caveat emptor! ("Let the buyer beware!")

Paying extra attention at the beginning of a commercial real estate transaction to *get it right* can save tens of thousands of dollars versus when the deal goes bad. It's like the old Fram oil filter slogan during the 1970s: "You can pay me now—or pay me later." In commercial real estate, however, *later* may be too late.

Buying commercial real estate is *not* like buying a home. It is not. It is not. It is *not*.

In Illinois, where my office is located, and in many other states, virtually every residential real estate closing requires a lawyer for the buyer and a lawyer for the seller. This is probably smart. It is good consumer protection.

The *problem* this causes, however, is that every lawyer handling residential real estate transactions considers himself or herself a *real estate lawyer* capable of handling any real estate transaction that may arise.

We learned in law school that there are only two kinds of property: real estate and personal property. Therefore—we intuit—if we are competent to handle a residential real estate closing, we must be competent to handle a commercial real estate closing. They are each *real estate*, right?

*Answer*: Yes, they are each real estate. No, they are not the same.

The legal issues and risks in a commercial real estate transaction are remarkably different from the legal issues and risks in a residential real estate transaction. Most are not even remotely similar. Attorneys concentrating their practice handling residential real estate closings do not face the same issues as attorneys concentrating their practice in commercial real estate.

It is a matter of experience. You either know the issues and risks inherent in commercial real estate transactions—and know how to deal with them—or you don't.

A key point to remember is that the myriad consumer-protection laws that protect residential home buyers have no application to—and provide no protection for—buyers of commercial real estate.

Competent commercial real estate practice requires focused and concentrated investigation of all issues material to the transaction by someone who knows what they are looking for. In short, it requires the exercise of due diligence.

I admit, the exercise of due diligence is not cheap, but the failure to exercise due diligence can create a financial disaster for the commercial real estate investor. Don't be *penny-wise and pound-foolish*.

If you are buying a home, hire an attorney who regularly represents home buyers. If you are buying commercial real estate, hire an attorney who regularly represents commercial real estate buyers.

Years ago, I stopped handling residential real estate transactions. As an active commercial real estate attorney, even I hire residential real estate counsel for my own home purchases. I do that because residential real estate practice is fundamentally different from commercial real estate.

Maybe I do *harp* on the need for competent counsel experienced in commercial real estate transactions. I genuinely believe it. I believe it is essential. I believe if you are going to invest in commercial real estate, you must apply your critical thinking skills and be smart.

*   *   *

*Pop quiz for you.* Here is a simple test of *your* critical thinking skills:

Please read the following scenarios and answer the questions *true* or *false*:

*Scenario number 1.* It's Valentine's Day. You are in hot pursuit of the love of your life. A few weeks ago, she confided in you that all she ever dreamed of for Valentine's Day was that her lover would show up at her door, dressed in a white tuxedo with tails and a top hat, and present her with a beautiful bouquet of flowers. You've rented the tuxedo, but now you are concerned about how much money you are spending.

*True or false.* Since flowers are pretty much all the same, it is OK for you to skip the roses and show up with a bouquet of fresh yellow dandelions.

*Scenario number 2.* For several years, your eyesight has deteriorated to the point where you can barely see your alarm clock. You are now considering corrective eye surgery so you won't need glasses. Your sister-in-law had corrective eye surgery and has had spectacular results. She recommends her eye surgeon but mentions the cost is about $5,700 for both eyes, and that the surgery is not covered by insurance. A few years ago, you had surgery to correct your hemorrhoids, and it cost you only $800.

*True or false.* Since surgeons all went to medical school and are all medical doctors, you are being frugal and wise by asking the surgeon who performed your hemorrhoid surgery to perform your corrective eye surgery.

*Scenario number 3.* Several years ago, when you first got married, you asked a former classmate who is a lawyer to represent you in the purchase of your townhome. The cost was only $375. A year later, you started a family and decided you needed a will. The same attorney prepared wills for you and your wife for a total cost of $700. You started your own business, and your attorney friend formed a corporation for you and charged you only $600 plus the cost of the corporate minute book. Years later, when your son was arrested for misdemeanor reckless driving, your attorney friend handled the criminal case and got your son off with supervision for only $1,500.

Your business has been successful, and you have built a pretty sizable nest egg, but you are tired of working for every dime and want to try investing in real estate. You have your eye on a strip shopping center. It includes a grocery store, bank, hardware store, dry cleaners (on a month-to-month tenancy), a couple of fast-food restaurants, a gift shop, dental office, bowling alley (with a lease about to expire), and wraps behind a gas station/mini-mart on the corner. The purchase price is $8 million, but the net operating income looks pretty good. You figure if you turn the bowling alley into a full-service restaurant/banquet facility and convert the dry cleaners into a twenty-four-hour coin laundry, the net operating income will increase, and the shopping center will turn into a spectacular investment. You plan to pull together much of your life savings and put down $2 million to buy this strip shopping center, borrowing the balance of $6 million. You remember that your lawyer friend handled the purchase of your home several years ago, so you know he handles real estate.

*True or false.* Commercial real estate is the same as residential real estate (hey, it's all dirt, isn't it?), so you are being a shrewd businessperson by hiring your lawyer friend who will charge much less than a lawyer who handles shopping center purchases several time a year. (What is this due diligence stuff anyway?)

## Answers

If you answered *true* for any of the foregoing scenarios, well, you have not been paying attention. Perhaps you should put this book down for a while and reflect on the course your life has taken.

If, on the other hand, you understand that the answer to each of the foregoing questions is *false*, I am available to help you in scenario number 3.

For scenario number 2, you should follow your sister-in-law's suggestion and contact her eye surgeon or some other eye surgeon with equal skill.

For scenario number 1, you are on your own. (But if you answered *true* for scenario number 1, you may be *forever* on you own.)

Investing in commercial real estate can be profitable and rewarding, but it requires use of critical thinking skills and competent counsel.

# 17

# Loan Workouts:
# Part 1—*Note to Lenders*

The advantages of pursuing a loan workout for defaulted loans can exist in good economic times and bad. In times of economy-wide distress, considering a loan workout can be critical to avoiding significant loss. The economy-wide slowdown that began in 2007, continued through 2008, and which appears likely to extend through 2009 and into 2010, and perhaps beyond, represents a case in point.

What began as a subprime residential loan calamity in March 2007 has spread to economy-wide weakness, impacting consumers and business alike. Commercial real estate loans and business loans are no exception. With the current economic stress, commercial real estate loans, including especially construction loans and development loans, and business loans generally, have been on an upward trend of default. The FDIC and other financial institution supervisory authorities have expressed concern. They have also expressed the need for close attention and creative problem solving to limit loan losses. Lenders should take heed.

Every commercial loan provides for legal and equitable remedies in the event of default. Lenders and their lawyers, accustomed to relying on the remedies contained in their loan documents, often do what is expected:

when a borrower falls behind on its payments or violates debt coverage ratios or other loan covenants, the lender declares a default, imposes an increased default rate of interest, accelerates the indebtedness, and commences foreclosure or other loan enforcement proceedings. The question is, under current economic conditions, does this make sense? The answer is *sometimes yes, sometimes no.* More and more frequently, the answer is no.

Think about it. The objective of loan enforcement is, or should be, to maximize recovery. In stable economic times, there may be many circumstances where it makes sense to follow the predictable enforcement scenario described above. When times are bad, a critical analysis must be made to calculate what action will, in fact, maximize recovery.

In tough economic times, with property values declining due to a glut of defaults, rising storefront vacancies, tightening credit standards, and skittish capital markets imposing higher yield requirements to offset rising risks, lenders must ask themselves, If I successfully foreclose this property, what am I going to do with it? What is my expected recovery? Declaring a default and mindlessly proceeding with foreclosure proceedings may be exactly the wrong solution.

There is a legal maxim that has equal application to lenders: "Ut vos reperio vestri in lacuna, subsisto fossura," which roughly translates to "When you find yourself in a hole, stop digging."

What works during good or even *normal* economic times may not make economic sense during an economic downturn.

To survive a sizable loan default during times of widespread economic weakness, a lender must think outside the box. The lender must focus on damage control. An elevated level of business acumen must be exercised.

The lender's underwriting criteria for loan origination may be irrelevant. What was required to originate the loan may not work now. Simple solutions are rarely at hand. The objective is to avoid, or at least minimize, loss. *Here's how*:

First and foremost, try to communicate with your borrower. Try to find out what is going on in the borrower's business that has resulted in this default. It is often more effective to look for solutions than it is to threaten the borrower with forced collection and foreclosure.

True. You may be annoyed that the borrower has not contacted you. Lack of communication raises suspicion and stress. The borrower *should* be contacting you, but this is no time to stand on ceremony.

Your borrower is likely under stress as well. Likely embarrassed he or she is not keeping up. Hoping against hope that things will turn around. If this loan is necessary for your borrower to stay in business, the borrower may be emotionally paralyzed into inaction with disbelief at the borrower's financial predicament. The borrower may be afraid to call you out of fear of humiliation. This may be especially true if the borrower has historically been successful in business. For your borrower, this is likely a new and traumatic experience.

I'm not pointing this out because I want you to feel sorry for the borrower. I'm pointing this out to help you understand the borrower's frame of mind and to put the loan default in context. This is not personal. Typically the borrower is not trying to rip you off. It is unlikely the borrower is using business proceeds to live the high life at your expense.

There are exceptions, sure. Part of what you need to do when a loan starts to lag in performance is to find out what is going on. If, in fact, the borrower is taking you for a ride by diverting funds to personal extravagances instead of paying your loan, then don't delay. Have a receiver appointed. Do what you must do to protect your collateral. In this case, your collateral may be a wasting asset. Time is your enemy.

Assuming this is not the case, however, and that borrower has just fallen on hard financial times, try to understand the nature of the problem. Is this just a temporary cash flow problem? Did the borrower's primary tenant or customer slow down its payments? Did a key tenant file bankruptcy or close its business due to economic stress? Has a government payer suspended payments while a new fiscal budget is approved? Has an unexpected rise in fuel costs or other costs soaked the profit out of a fixed-term vendor contract the borrower is obligated to perform?

If the borrower's cash flow problems are temporary, does it make sense to declare a default and compound the borrower's problems? Will this maximize *your* recovery?

If you work with the borrower, can the borrower pull through the current economic distress and get back on track? Does it make sense to extend the borrower a temporary working capital line of credit or increase an existing line of credit to solve borrower's current cash crunch? Lending a borrower additional funds when the borrower is in default may seem counterintuitive, but will it increase your likelihood of achieving a full recovery? What are your chances of recovery if you don't?

Is a loan modification agreement appropriate? What about extending the repayment schedule? Or reducing, instead of increasing, the borrower's effective interest rate? This does not necessarily mean actually reducing the borrower's rate of interest, but perhaps agreeing to reduce the amount payable currently and accruing the rest.

Consider an example where the loan rate is 8% and the default rate is 12%. If the borrower is experiencing cash flow problems that have resulted in borrower's inability to remain current with payments based on a loan rate of 8%, is it reasonable to think the borrower will be able to keep up with payments if the interest rate is increased to 12%?

In a loan default setting, one of the most misapplied financial maxims is "higher risk requires a higher rate of return." This maxim is used as one of the justifications for applying a higher interest rate in the case of default. There is no question a loan in default presents a high financial risk.

While there is a reason to provide for a higher default interest rate, this is not it. The valid reason is to serve as a disincentive for default. But where a default is beyond the practical control of the borrower, should it necessarily be imposed?

The "higher risk, higher rate" maxim is really a principle of capital attraction. To *attract* capital for debt or equity financing, higher risk really does require a higher rate of return. Unless you are selling your defaulted loan, however, attracting capital is not the issue. You have already funded your loan. Your task now is to maximize recovery.

At the very least, you need to recover your principal. If you can recover your costs of collection and accrued interest, better still. Ideally, you will recover it all, including your higher rate of accrued default interest. Recognize, however, that what is ideal may not be what is realistic. Once again, the guiding light is maximizing recovery. Sometimes making a profit is not an option. Minimizing loss may be the only viable strategy.

If you review the borrower's financial condition and determine the borrower's cash flow difficulties are temporary, instead of increasing payments to cover 12% default interest, consider whether it would make more sense to base payments on 4% and accrue the other 8% until the borrower's cash flow situation improves.

If you determine the borrower's cash flow difficulties are permanent and the best solution is to liquidate the collateral, consider whether you will recover more through a foreclosure sale or through sale as a going concern. What do you need to do to facilitate the sale as a going concern? Who should run your borrower's property or business in the meantime? Is the extra cost of appointing a receiver or trustee going to result in a greater recovery for you?

On numerous occasions, I have dealt with lenders who insist on rigidly sticking to their original lending criteria. Frequently, the lender demands that the borrower raise more capital to cure borrower's default and restore lender's required loan ratios. This is a great solution for the lender if it is possible. The question to ask is, how realistic is it, and will it really solve the underlying financial difficulties? If the borrower does not have its own funds to invest, where is the additional capital supposed to come from?

Recalling the maxim for capital attraction stated above, what rate of return will prospective investors require to induce them to inject more capital into the borrower's already-struggling enterprise? How will this high rate of return be realized? What impact will that have on the borrower's future prospects for loan compliance? In the long run, will this strategy improve or impair your chances for full recovery?

In every case, the lender's mantra should be maximize recovery, maximize recovery, maximize recovery. Every lender decision after default should be focused on this objective. The path to maximum recovery may not be obvious and, in some cases, may seem counterintuitive. Still, it must be your guiding light.

As we start down the path of considering a loan workout, it is essential that we obtain a clear and accurate picture of the borrower's true financial circumstances. If you are not sure about the quality of financial information we are getting from your borrower, consider requiring that the borrower engage an independent financial consultant. The consultant should be professional and qualified. The consultant must understand that although he or she is being paid by the borrower, the consultant owes a fiduciary duty to accurately report to the lender.

Fortunately, there are a lot of qualified professional financial consultants. Among my favorites in Chicago, Illinois, are Nancy A. Ross and Tina L. Hughes of High Ridge Partners Inc. (*www.high-ridge.com*), John C. Wheeler of DSI—Development Specialists Inc. (*www.dsi.biz*), Steve Baer of Rally Capital Services LLC (*www.rallyllc.com*), and Donald Shapiro of Foresite Realty Partners LLC (*www.foresiterealty.com*). They are never cheap, but they are often worth the added expense. Be sure the one you pick knows your borrower's business or can learn it very quickly. Require a strict and frequent reporting schedule. If you determine the borrower's financial situation is not going to improve, be ready to pull the plug and do what you have to do to maximize your recovery.

If the borrower won't voluntarily agree to engage a financial consultant, go ahead and declare a default; then require employment of a financial consultant as a condition to entry into a forbearance agreement. A forbearance agreement is a good idea in all events. It should include an acknowledgment of the loan default and a waiver of defenses as conditions to your agreeing to work with the borrower to try to find an amicable solution to the borrower's financial crisis.

While you gather information and work with the borrower, have an attorney review your loan file to make sure you have everything you need in the event you must resort to forced collection and foreclosure. It may surprise you how often your documentation is incomplete or inaccurate. At a minimum, make sure your note, mortgage, security agreement, and guaranties are signed, that the mortgage is recorded, and your security interest is perfected.

What is the value of that personal guaranty now? Require current financial statements from the borrower and each guarantor. Determine whether the borrower has additional capital available or additional collateral to pledge to fully secure your loan. Make sure all necessary corporate resolutions and other authority documents are executed and in your loan file.

As you work with the borrower, you must always consider the risk that the borrower may file bankruptcy. Understand the consequences.

Bankruptcy proceedings are often very expensive. For this reason, they may degrade rather than enhance your recovery even as a secured lender. Perhaps to your surprise, being oversecured can create nearly as many problems in bankruptcy as being undersecured. The problems are not exactly the same, but each has its own challenges.

If your loan is undersecured, you will likely be treated as a general unsecured creditor for that portion exceeding the value of your collateral. To avoid this risk, it is not uncommon for some lenders to proceed to the opposite extreme of grossly oversecuring their loans. This strategy, while in the long run preferable to being undersecured, is not without issues.

In cases where the borrower has significantly oversecured its loan, a bankruptcy judge has the authority to significantly reduce or suspend the borrower's obligation to make current debt service payments by determining the lender is adequately protected by the value of its collateral. That can mean no payments whatsoever on your loan while the bankruptcy is pending. If the cash flow from loan repayment is important to the lender, this could create a serious problem.

The point of all this, for lenders, is that to maximize your loan recovery, you must exercise good business judgment. Blind adherence to conventional remedies for breach of contract may not be your best answer. Be creative and focus on what will maximize your recovery under the unique circumstances of this particular loan default with this particular collateral and this particular borrower.

While doing this, do it in a way that does not expose you to lender liability. At all times you must maintain your role as a lender acting responsibly to maximize your recovery. Avoid any action that may transform you into a role tantamount to that of a business partner. This is not difficult but may sometimes require you to walk a fine line.

Taking a creative approach to loan defaults and focusing on ways to work with your borrower are often essential elements to minimizing loan losses and maximizing recovery. This is the essence of an effective loan workout.

# 18

# Loan Workouts: Part 2—*Note to Borrowers*

Thirty years ago, a classmate of mine went to work for a law firm specializing in mortgage foreclosures. His pet name for defaulted borrowers was *mooches*. His philosophy was that defaulted borrowers were basically crooks. They had taken his client's money and wouldn't pay it back. The distinction between unwillingness to repay and inability to repay didn't matter to him. Changes in circumstances didn't matter to him. To his mind (what little of it there was), it was as clear as night and day: the mooches were no better than thieves. He was out for blood. To him, it was personal.

Unfortunately, we still sometimes deal with lenders and attorneys like my former classmate. They would rather punish a defaulted borrower than work to maximize their recovery. For them, a loan workout is a sign of weakness. With them, a voluntary loan workout may be difficult. We can try to work with these lenders and their attorneys to show them how the lender may be better off taking a less adversarial approach, but like it or not, lenders—like defaulted borrowers—don't always make rational choices. Fortunately, however, they usually do. Sophisticated lenders with sophisticated lender's counsel understand that in a loan default scenario, the primary objective is to maximize the lender's recovery and recognize that the path to maximum recovery may not be as obvious as it might seem.

If you are a borrower reading this, perhaps your business or commercial development is in financial distress, or you want to prepare yourself in case matters get worse. I understand. These are tough economic times. Unless you have faced a severe financial crisis before, there is little reason to know much about this topic.

You are not alone. Although you may have never before experienced financial distress at a level that has caused you to default on an important real estate or business loan, structural changes in our economy and other financial stresses outside the control of borrowers do take their toll. It does not make you a bad person or necessarily suggest you have exercised poor business judgment. Sometimes a good business decision under one set of circumstances becomes a disaster when conditions change. Unfortunately, your business or commercial investment is where the pain of adverse change is felt. Bitter consequences may become unavoidable. To paraphrase a cliché, in times of economic trouble, your business or real estate development is where the rubber meets the road.

Speaking of rubber, that's a perfect example. I represented a client recently that manufactured rubber and plastic toys for large retailers. The way that business works is that manufacturers contract in January or February to deliver their rubber and plastic toys to retailers between August and November, in time for the Christmas shopping season. The wholesale price per unit is agreed upon at the time the contract is executed. The toys are then manufactured between March and October. It's a pretty good system. The product is presold before being manufactured. The risk of being stuck with an inventory of unsold toys is minimal. For many years, this system worked perfectly.

As you may have guessed, the unexpected and drastic rise in petroleum prices created a problem. In case you don't know, rubber and plastic are petroleum-based products. The cost of manufacturing rubber and plastic products has always fluctuated to some extent based upon the world market price for crude oil. The customary market risk of small price fluctuations was factored into the delivery price. What was not factored in was the sudden dramatic rise in crude oil prices we have experienced over the recent past. As a consequence, what began as a built-in profit turned into a built-in loss. It's not surprising that this client fell on hard economic times and defaulted on its loans. Did that mean the client's managers were bad people? Does it even mean they used poor business judgment? Beyond these questions is the important one: how do we best deal with the client's defaulted real estate and business loans?

As another example, consider the client who for generations has been in the wholesale bakery business. It's a huge business. The client's bakery goods are sold in grocery stores and convenience stores throughout the United States.

Financial difficulties arose, but not from an economic recession or rising costs of raw materials. This client's problems arose from a book, a diet book of all things: *Dr. Atkins' New Diet Revolution.* You may recall it was the rage a few years back. The fundamental premise of the Atkins diet is that carbohydrates are bad and will make you fat. Never mind that good nutrition and losing weight involve more than just cutting carbohydrates; that was the premise of the Atkins diet, and consumers bought into it big-time.

A consequence of the Atkins diet was that consumers greatly reduced their intake of bakery products, a key source of carbohydrates. Bakery sales dropped precipitously. Bakers with high fixed costs suffered unprecedented losses. Does this make bakery owners poor businesspeople? Did this foreshadow the end of the bakery industry? We don't hear much about the Atkins diet anymore. It was a temporary consumer phenomenon. The bakery industry is on the rebound.

I'm not relating these examples because misery loves company. My purpose is to give you a frame of reference as you prepare for discussions with your lender. And discuss, you must.

One of the most fundamental mistakes borrowers make is failure to communicate with their lender. The strategy many borrowers seem to follow is one of beat the clock. The premise seems to be that somehow, someway, their financial distress will be resolved before their lender notices they are falling behind. The obvious question is, how? What will be different tomorrow than it is today? Do you really think your financial problem will fix itself in the next thirty days? How exactly is that to occur? Unless you have an ironclad financial solution that is virtually certain to occur (for instance, your two-year jumbo CD is maturing next week at which time you will liquidate the CD and pay off the loan or, at least, inject sufficient funds to overcome your financial woes), communication is essential. Even when you have an ironclad solution, communication is a good idea.

I understand you may be embarrassed. For a businessperson accustomed to success, facing a loan default is a humbling experience. It can be a hard conversation to have. The alternative, however, can be worse. Failure to communicate raises suspicion and doubt.

If you have an ironclad solution, acknowledge to your lender that you have a temporary cash flow problem and explain how you are going to fix it. For this to work, however, you must carry through and actually fix your problem. Acknowledging a problem then fixing it tends to build lender confidence in a borrower. Trust is a valuable resource. Acknowledging a problem and suggesting a solution that does not come to pass has the opposite effect.

If you do not have an ironclad solution you are certain will come to pass in the immediate future, your best course is to take an alternative approach. That approach is the loan workout.

In a loan workout, you acknowledge you have a financial problem, then seek the lender's indulgence as you strive to fix the problem over time. The amount of time a lender may be willing to work with you will depend on two things: (1) the lender's confidence that your solution will really work and (2) belief by your lender that it will not be worse off by waiting to foreclose.

Each of these is important, but the second is likely most important. The lender is interested in maximizing its recovery. It does not want to lose money any more than you do. If there is a substantial risk that your lender will recover less if it delays enforcement, your lender will not likely wait.

Your lender's level of confidence that the solution will really work likewise depends on two factors: (i) your lender's confidence in the solution and (ii) your lender's confidence in you and your ability to implement the solution.

If you can't convince your lender that the solution you propose is viable, your loan workout efforts will go nowhere. Likewise, if you can't demonstrate to your lender that it will likely recover more if it works with you than if it pursues default remedies, forbearance from your lender is unlikely. Finally, if your lender does not trust your ability and commitment to carry out the solution, the lender will not likely wait to start enforcement proceedings.

Understand that from the lender's perspective, the loan default is really not about you. It is about the lender. What is the best course of action for the lender?

You may think this is unfair. You may believe that because you have been a loyal and profitable customer to the lender over time, the lender should bend over backward to help you even if its risk of loss is rising. The hard news is it's not going to happen. It doesn't work that way. The only reason a lender may even consider the fact that you have been a loyal and profitable customer is if the lender believes there is still more profit to be made from you in the future. Commercial lending is a business. Lenders don't stay in business by voluntarily losing money.

Likewise, from your perspective, the loan default and loan workout are really not about the lender. As a defaulting borrower, finding a solution for a loan default is about what is in your best interests. If you have no financial exposure and little or nothing to gain by working through the loan default, it's a good bet you won't. On the other hand, if you have substantial equity invested or you have personally guaranteed the loan to your lender, you will likely work to do what is necessary to pay off the lender, but not for the lender's sake, for your own sake.

The reason a loan workout is even plausible is because in many situations, what is good for the borrower is also good for the lender—at least to some degree. Since a secured lender will get its money before you get your equity, actions that protect your equity are typically beneficial to the lender. Beware, however, that the converse is not necessarily true. Since a secured lender will be paid before you receive your equity and before you are relieved from liability under your guaranty, a lender may well choose to sacrifice your interests to protect its own.

What does this mean to you? It means you have to structure a solution that protects your lender so your lender will give you time to save yourself. It also means you have to watch your backside while pursuing a financial solution.

To do this, you need to evaluate and understand all your legal options. Determine any defenses you may have to enforcement of the loan or enforcement of your personal guaranty, any viable claims you may have against your lender that may lead to lender liability, the benefits and burdens of filing for bankruptcy protection and how that will likely affect your lender; and you must calculate the lender's recovery risk if you stop operating and the lender is forced to foreclose on its collateral rather than being able to sell the collateral as part of a going concern. Be prepared to use all the tools and remedies at your disposal to motivate the lender to proceed in a manner that protects your interests while reasonably protecting its own.

Understand, however, that any solution you devise to protect your interests must be a viable solution that protects the lender as well. This is the only basis upon which the lender will cooperate in a loan workout. Like it or not, if the loan was properly documented and adequately secured, and provided the lender has not taken any overt actions that expose it to a legitimate lender liability claim, the secured lender has the upper hand.

## The Seven Principles of Loan Workout Negotiations

The following principles of loan workout negotiation are, for this chapter, presented from the perspective of the borrower; but they apply equally to the lender. To apply them from the lender's perspective, simply substitute *lender* for *borrower* and vice versa.

## *The Borrower's Loan Workout Principles*

1. To get what you want, you must give the lender what it needs.
2. What the lender needs is often less than what the lender wants.
3. What the borrower wants is often more than the borrower actually needs.
4. Borrower and lender often don't need as much as they believe they need.
5. The loan workout objective must be for each party to get all that it actually needs and, if possible, some of what it wants.
6. It is in the overlap of what the borrower and lender want above what they legitimately need that there is room for compromise.

7. To effectively negotiate a loan workout, it is essential for each party to have a realistic understanding of its actual bottom-line needs and the actual bottom-line needs of the other. To *win* the loan workout negotiation, you allow the lender to get all what it needs while you get most of what you want.

Borrowers and lenders typically have a clear understanding of what they want as they enter into a loan workout negotiation. Unfortunately, they often fail to acknowledge, even to themselves, their actual bottom-line needs. Even when they have clearly analyzed their own needs, they seldom have the insight or willingness to analyze and understand the other party's actual bottom-line needs.

To make loan workout negotiations even more challenging, even when a party clearly understands its own bottom-line needs, it is not uncommon to withhold that information from their representative negotiating on their behalf often out of fear their representative will settle for less than what they want.

While I don't recommend this approach, it is not necessarily fatal. It can become fatal to the loan workout negotiation process, however, when what you insist is your bottom-line need prevents the other party from getting what it needs. It can then become what is aptly referred to as a *deal killer*.

To most effectively and successfully negotiate a loan workout, three tactical elements are recommended.

The first is to negotiate through a representative. This creates a buffer that allows hard-fought positions to be compromised when necessary with minimal damage to the credibility of your negotiator. This is critical because a large part of any successful negotiation is credibility with the other party, which requires conscientious trust building to convince the lender you are acting in good faith.

Second, be sure you select a skilled and knowledgeable negotiator you trust to work diligently in your best interests; then be open and honest with your negotiator as to what you want and what you actually need. This is important because effective negotiation requires flexibility and creativity to maneuver the negotiation to a successful conclusion. If your negotiator does not know what you actually need as compared to what you merely want, opportunities to maximize your benefit may be lost through unnecessary intransigence as to your stated positions.

Third, have a workable plan B. If you do not have a workable plan B, you are at a tremendous disadvantage in bargaining power.

Make no mistake. Negotiating a loan workout is not an easy way out. Any and all expenses the lender incurs will be yours to pay. That includes attorney's fees—both the lender's and your own—fees of inspectors, fees of consultants, fees of accountants to examine your books and records, fees of a financial agent to monitor your cash flow, fees of title insurance companies, and every other expense reasonably incurred to collect the debt.

This is one more reason to look for real solutions that will take hold quickly and have a substantial likelihood of success. Your collateral may be a wasting asset that is declining in value by reason of your default. Your lender won't wait long for you to find and implement a solution.

The legal maxim I suggested to lenders in "Loan Workouts: Part 1—Note to Lenders" applies equally to borrowers: "Ut vos reperio vestry in lacuna, subsisto fossura," which roughly translates to "When you find yourself in a hole, stop digging."

If there is no viable solution to your financial disaster, stop digging. You are only getting yourself deeper in debt.

This does not mean, however, that you should stop searching for a viable solution when you are merely on a downward slide. Finding a way to preserve your investment, or at least minimize your losses, makes perfect business sense. Understanding how to do this requires knowledge and experience. Seek competent help if you need it.

# 19

# ECOA Compliance: Commercial Banks at Risk

Remarkably, a number of banks, particularly smaller community banks, but regional, national and international banks as well, continue to expose themselves to substantial risks of civil liability for noncompliance with the Equal Credit Opportunity Act (ECOA). The ECOA provides that a bank or other covered creditor that fails to comply with a requirement imposed by ECOA or Regulation B (12 CFR 202) is subject to civil liability for actual and punitive damages in individual or class actions. Liability for punitive damages can be as high as $10,000 in individual actions and the lesser of $500,000 or 1% of net worth in class actions. Further, the ECOA authorizes the awarding of costs and reasonable attorney's fees to an aggrieved applicant in a successful action.

How common are violations of the ECOA that may result in these potentially catastrophic damages? For many banks, much more common than one might imagine.

For years, it was second nature and a common lending practice to require a *spouse's signature* on business loans.

A husband might come into a bank for a loan to purchase or finance a business or commercial building or other commercial enterprise. Though his credit was good and the collateral sufficient, at closing the bank would require his wife to sign a guarantee or cosign the note. A typical rationale was that the lender didn't want the borrower to be able to *hide* assets in his wife's name.

Similarly, in the past, it has not been uncommon for a bank to require the guarantee of a husband when a married businesswoman sought commercial financing. How many times has a woman sought a loan to operate a restaurant, a jewelry store, a hair salon, a light manufacturing business, or other traditionally viewed "woman's business" only to be told she needs her husband's guarantee even when her own credit is good and her collateral sufficient?

Somewhat surprisingly, this mentality persists today, though the practice is clearly unlawful.

The ECOA, and Regulation B (12 CFR 202) promulgated to implement the ECOA, makes clear that the historical practice of requiring a spouse's signature on a loan as a matter of course is contrary to law and can result in substantial civil liability to a bank or other covered lender.

Regulation B expressly provides that the purpose of this regulation is to promote the availability of credit to all creditworthy applicants without regard to: race, color, religion, national origin, sex, marital status, or age (provided the applicant has the capacity to contract); to the fact that all or a part of the applicant's income derives from a public assistance program; or to the fact that the applicant has in good faith exercised any right under the Consumer Credit Protection Act. The regulation prohibits creditor practices that discriminate on the basis of any of these factors. The regulation also requires creditors to notify applicants of action taken on their applications, to report credit history in the names of both spouses on an account; to retain records of credit applications; to collect information about the applicant's race and other personal characteristics in applications for certain dwelling-related loans; and to provide applicants with copies of appraisal reports used in connection with credit transactions. (12 CFR 202.1[b])

An express FDIC examination point included in part 3 of the *FDIC Compliance Manual* outlining examination procedures for ECOA fair lending requires, consistent with 12 CFR 202.5(c)(2), that information concerning a spouse or former spouse ("Spouse") of an applicant must not be required by a creditor unless (i) the spouse will be a user of, or contractually liable on, the account; (ii) the applicant is relying upon the credit of the spouse's income to repay the debt; (iii) the applicant resides in a community property state or is relying upon property located in a community property state as a basis for repayment of the requested credit, or the applicant is relying on alimony, child support, or separate maintenance to repay the debt. (*Note*, for example, Illinois, Indiana, and Florida are NOT community property states; New Mexico and California are community property states.)

As an example of failure to comply with this requirement, one of my clients recently applied for a business loan to purchase a commercial building, and the business and inventory operated from within the building. The applicant owned another successful business and had good individual credit. The applicant's spouse was not placed on title to the commercial building or vested with any ownership rights or interest in the business or inventory. She was not *offered* by the applicant as an additional obligor to support his credit application; and in fact, by all objective measures, his own credit was sufficient to qualify him for the loan. Notwithstanding these facts, the lender, a large bank with offices in the Chicago region, required that the applicant's spouse guarantee the loan as a condition to funding.

Though this applicant has chosen to ignore this clear violation of the ECOA out of fear an objection may impair his future business and credit relationship with this lender, this lender has exposed itself to civil liability to the applicant for actual damages, punitive damages, and attorney's fees, as well as regulatory sanction from bank examiners. One might only imagine the challenge this lender will face if the applicant defaults and the lender seeks to enforce the loan, including the spouse's guarantee.

In fact, in a separate and completely unrelated transaction, this same lender similarly required a spouse of another borrower to guaranty a construction loan for a large condominium project. The spouse was not offered by the borrower as additional credit support, and the loan was approved by the lender without considering the spouse's credit, but with an added condition that the spouse sign a guaranty of the loan.

The lender has now filed suit to foreclose the loan and to enforce the guaranty against the principal borrower and his spouse. The bank's violation of ECOA has been raised as a defense to the bank's effort to enforce the spouse's guaranty. Unless we are able to negotiate a favorable settlement for the benefit of our client, our intent is to seek to have the spouse's guaranty declared invalid and unenforceable based upon the bank's violation of the Equal Credit Opportunity Act. This would put the spouse's substantial assets out of the reach of the bank for collection of this debt. If successful, the principal borrower plans to file bankruptcy, making collection doubtful. We have also prepared a counterclaim against the bank seeking monetary damages, attorney's fees, and statutory punitive damages.

If nothing else, this lender's violation of ECOA has turned a rather routine foreclosure and guaranty enforcement proceeding into a hotly contested dispute that may prevent the lender from holding the spouse liable. It may additionally expose the lender to liability for damages and attorneys' fees. It will almost certainly prevent the lender from quick resolution of the litigation through summary judgment.

To avoid this clear exposure to liability, it is paramount that commercial banks and other lenders sensitize themselves to the mandates of the ECOA and Regulation B. Compliance must become second nature. Comprehensive assessment of lending systems must take place.

The "old days" of commercial lending are gone. From credit application to credit funding or denial of credit and beyond, lenders must be aware of this liability risk and beware its consequences.

**20**

# The Time to Decide: Commercial Litigation

A sage once said, "The time to worry about where the ball will drop is before the wheel is spun." He was speaking about roulette, of course, but the wisdom of these words has much broader application. The point is, worry about the outcome before you place the bet when you can still do something about it.

Commercial litigation, especially commercial real estate litigation, is in some respects like roulette. Once your lawsuit is filed, the wheel is spinning. Unlike roulette, you may still have a measure of control over the outcome, but you are in it until the ball drops.

In commercial litigation, there is seldom an insurance company prepared to write a check. There is a substantial risk the case will proceed to trial. There is no guaranty you will collect anything—especially if payment of money is not the relief you seek. Consequently, there is very little chance your attorney will accept your commercial dispute on a contingent fee basis. A third of nothing is still nothing.

Lawyers handling commercial litigation are not your partners. Commercial litigators charge by the hour. Except in rare cases where you can negotiate a hybrid fee arrangement, you will assume the entire financial risk—not your lawyer. Your lawyer is serving as your paid professional advocate, a hired gun, so to speak.

As long as you are willing and able to pay your lawyer to apply his or her skill and training to your cause, your lawyer is bound to represent you with zeal and vigor. If you do not pay, you should expect your lawyer to stop work. The fact that the practice of law is a profession does not make it a charitable enterprise. It is both a profession and a business. There is no moral or ethical imperative for a lawyer to work without pay while advocating a commercial dispute. Commercial litigation is business litigation, and the business being advanced is yours.

I am not a big fan of commercial litigation. It is expensive for my clients and distracts them from their core business. It is in their core business where they make money. It is because of their core business that I am their lawyer. Still, if you are going to litigate, then commit to litigate. Do not file a lawsuit unless you intend to see it through and win.

If you know anything about law firm profitability, it may surprise you to hear me say I am not a huge fan of litigation. Lawsuits can be very profitable for lawyers. Lawsuits are labor intensive and can take on a life of their own. Huge legal fees can be run up in a hurry. If that is how you determine to spend your money, then, by all means, call me. My law firm has an outstanding group of litigators. In commercial litigation, we combine our transactional knowledge with litigation prowess and are unsurpassed. I just think you ought to make an informed and seriously calculated decision before you decide to spend your money in this way.

It is virtually impossible to predict with accuracy how much a lawsuit will cost. Typically, it will cost much more than you imagine. This is because unlike a business or real estate transaction you can choose to walk away from if it ceases to make economic sense, lawsuits, once filed, are not so easy to escape. It's like choosing to dance with an eight-hundred-pound gorilla. As the joke goes, "When do you stop? When the gorilla decides to stop." Once you have filed a lawsuit or have taken a position in a dispute that will lead to your adversary filing a lawsuit, you have reached the dance floor and may very well find yourself cheek to cheek with an eight-hundred-pound gorilla.

Don't get me wrong. There are times when litigation is necessary and appropriate. There are times when an adversary is so brazenly interfering with your business or trampling on your rights and interests that the benefits of litigation will far exceed your costs. There are times when litigation is your only reasonable choice.

In making the decision to proceed, however, understand the tangible and intangible costs. Attorneys' fees may run into tens of thousands of dollars and, in a complicated case, perhaps even into the hundreds of thousands of dollars. The litigation may also distract you from your core business and subject you to significant emotional strain and sleepless nights. Do not underestimate these add-on intangible costs.

If you are going to litigate, be sure to hire a lawyer experienced in the type of litigation you intend to pursue. Litigation strategy is based on game theory. Each move you make must anticipate your adversary's next several moves. Your strategy and its implementation must be designed to win and be agile enough to adapt to changing circumstances if your adversary moves forward in an unanticipated way. Knowledge is power.

Part of what makes litigation emotionally draining is a lack of understanding about how the process works. It is not as mysterious as clients sometimes seem to believe.

The bones of litigation are this: You and your adversary are in disagreement. You are convinced your position is superior. Your adversary is convinced its position is superior. You are unable to reach a compromise that works for you both. Filing a lawsuit is a decision to let someone else decide.

The litigation process is a process of gathering useful information to support your position and to undermine your opponent's position. Your adversary is engaged in the same process. Some of this information is applicable law. Much of the information is supporting facts. Ultimately, you will each present your compiled information to an independent decision maker. A judge or jury will decide.

Proceeding with commercial litigation can be both time-consuming and expensive. If you are going to litigate, the decision to do so should be based upon a sober determination of the benefits likely to be achieved, the costs of obtaining those benefits, and your likelihood of success. You may have the greatest case in the world, your lawyer may tell you it will be a *slam dunk*, but if it is going to cost you more than you reasonably expect to gain—measuring both tangible and intangible costs—at least consider the choice of not proceeding. The decision to proceed or not to proceed is yours. It is very much a business decision.

In making the decision to litigate, use the same skills of economic analysis you use to make real estate investment decisions. If you know it will cost you $2 million to develop and market a project, but your likely return is only $1.5 million, would you proceed? If your disputed claim is for $50,000, but it will cost you $60,000 to $100,000 to collect, should you proceed? The answer may depend upon other factors as well, but all else being equal, the rational economic choice is obvious.

Too often lawsuits are filed as an emotional response to a perceived slight rather than being based upon an objective determination that the lawsuit is in your best economic interest. Do not let elevated testosterone levels get in the way of making a rational economic decision. The lawsuit is likely to continue long after your passions have faded. By that time, you may be wrapped in the arms of that eight-hundred-pound gorilla. If you have not made the decision to litigate based upon legitimate and dispassionate commercial considerations, you may find that your only way out is to settle on highly unfavorable terms. This will not help you prosper.

A common mistake clients make is to assume that if a dispute is over only $10,000 to $50,000, the attorneys' fees for pursuing or defending the case will be proportionately less than if the lawsuit involved $100,000 to $1 million. This is not necessarily so. The amount of time it takes to prove your case has very little to do with the amount in dispute. The facts and issues and the response of your adversary determine the amount of time involved. Since commercial litigation is typically billed by the hour, more time means higher attorneys' fees regardless of the amount in dispute. This reality should be taken into consideration when deciding to file suit and likewise when considering an offer of settlement.

Some protection may be provided by the documents if they provide for the successful party to recover attorneys' fees and costs from the unsuccessful party. But note: (i) you had better be sure you will be the successful party, or you may end up paying your adversary's attorneys' fees as well as your own; and (ii) you should consider whether a judgment against this particular defendant is likely to be collected. If the defendant is on the verge of bankruptcy or otherwise insolvent, obtaining a judgment that includes all your attorneys' fees will do you little good.

Remember. The commercial dispute forming the basis of your lawsuit is yours, not your attorney's. Your attorney's business is to represent you as your skilled professional advocate. Attorneys are bound to zealously advocate for your success, but they cannot guaranty success and collection.

Deciding to file a lawsuit in a commercial dispute should be like deciding to get a kidney transplant. It should be a decision that is not entered into lightly and should be made only if the benefits to be obtained are greater than the burdens the procedure will entail. If you decide on a new kidney and go under the knife, be prepared to see it through. If, after the procedure has begun and your kidney has been removed, you change your mind and decide against a transplant, your decision is a bit too late. The time to make that decision was before you got on the operating table.

I am not saying you should never file a lawsuit. Each circumstance merits its own evaluation. What I am saying is that the time to decide is *before* the suit is filed. Once filed, be prepared to do what must be done to win. It is too late to unspin the wheel.

# 21

# Brass Tacks

My grandfather, affectionately referred to as W. E., was sharp as a tack. He was a gruff, no-nonsense kind of guy. He died when I was young but left a legacy of practicality when it came to getting things done.

I can still remember warm summer evenings sitting on the deck of his cabin cruiser, anchored in the Green River just off the Ohio with four or five lines in the water, a stringer of smelly catfish in a bucket, and W. E. chomping on his Cuban cigar, talking with my father and uncle about pressing family business. I was just a kid, so I didn't pay a whole lot of attention; but I can remember him barking out his favorite phrase, "Let's get down to brass tacks!" That was his way of saying, "Enough with the generalities already, how exactly are we going to get this done?" What *this* was didn't matter. If there was unfinished business, he wanted facts and a specific plan to get it done.

It wasn't until years later that I recognized what a powerful influence W. E. had been on my father and his brother and our family as a whole. We are ingrained, almost by heredity, to "get down to brass tacks."

So here we go. Throughout most of this book up to this point, I have spoken in generalities. Each chapter has been largely about process, a general way of approaching commercial real estate. But as W.E. would say, we have to get down to brass tacks.

Just as most of the first part of this book was about process, most of the balance of this book will be about specifics. If you are serious about investing in commercial real estate, you need to know some, if not all, of what follows.

By necessity, I will, to some extent, be discussing select tax laws and various Supreme Court and appellate court cases. But don't worry. What follows is not a legal textbook. This book is written for developers and investors. Our property system is founded on laws, however, some of which you need to know. Commercial real estate is a favorite focus for taxes and tax incentives. Taxes to finance government and tax incentives to encourage investors and developers to invest in the kinds of real estate projects our government finds worthy of promotion. To really prosper in commercial real estate, you need to know about these things and how to use them to your advantage to maximize your return.

Many of the citations I will give are federal. That means they apply in every state. In other cases, I will refer to the laws of a specific state, usually Illinois since that is where my legal practice is concentrated. Don't feel these citations are entirely irrelevant if you are not investing in Illinois. Property laws and tax incentives may vary from state to state, but often not by much. If your attorney is unfamiliar with a particular tax incentive discussed in this book, it is not particularly difficult for him or her to do a bit of research to find out if similar tax incentives are available in your state. If your attorney does not know they exist, your attorney will not know what to look for. If a tax incentive is available in Illinois, there is a good chance the same tax incentive, or something very similar, will be available in most of the other forty-nine states.

If you want to do your own preliminary research, try searching the key phrases and concepts referred to in the cases I cite by using a free Internet search engine. I usually use Google. Type in the key words or concepts and add your state. For example, if you are interested in whether your state law allows use of tax increment financing to finance brownfield development and cleanup, try typing in key words, such as **tax increment financing, brownfield development, (your state)**. If you are interested in brownfield development tax credits, try typing in key words such as **brownfield development, tax credits, (your state)**. It's not a perfect search tool, but you may be surprised what you come up with.

Also, it should go without saying, but do not believe everything you read on the Internet. Much of it has not been vetted for accuracy or reliability. If it sounds too good to be true, there is likely more to it than meets the eye. Do your due diligence. Get to the meat of it. Confirm what you read with in-depth examination and analysis using your critical thinking skills. The statutory and case law citations in the following chapters are included for this purpose.

One final point I need to make to keep my tax partners from falling out of their chairs is inclusion of what has come to be known as the *IRS Circular 230 Disclosure.*

As required by the Internal Revenue Service under Circular 230, you are advised that any U.S. federal tax advice contained in this book is not intended or written to be used, and cannot be used, for the purpose of (i) avoiding penalties under the Internal Revenue Code or (ii) promoting, marketing or recommending to another party any transaction or matter addressed in this book.

Also, the tax discussions in this book are not intended as legal advice. You should consult your own tax advisor if you have any particular questions as to how tax laws may apply to your particular situation. You can contact me if you'd like, and I will put you in touch with one of my tax partners. Just don't treat this book as a legal opinion regarding your specific tax situation.

OK, with that out of the way, let's get down to brass tacks.

**22**

# Turning Brownfields Green

We've all seen it. That perfect corner location, vacant industrial building, or urban site that just seems to sit empty year after year. *"Environmental problem,"* we hear. *"Costs too much to clean up." "They can't give that site away."*

Perhaps.

What if the site were clean? Would it be a good development site then? What if instead of environmental cleanup costs coming out of your pocket, you could get the government to pay them? What if, additionally, you could get income tax deductions or, better yet, transferable income tax credits for cleaning up the site?

Government funds may not be available in every case, but when government funds are available, commercial real estate projects not otherwise feasible can be made profitable. For developers, profitable is good.

## The Case for Government Incentives
## for Brownfield Development

Developers and investors hear about other developers and investors receiving government money to pay for portions of their project and want to know how to get their share. There are many circumstances and conditions that will qualify a project and its developer to receive public money. In this chapter, we will talk about that.

As we shall see, the key to receiving public money for private development is a determination by governmental officials that the private development achieves a public purpose. This can be tricky and will often require an in-depth professional study of the project area, the project particulars, and its expected benefits to the community. These are serious studies that must be undertaken by qualified professionals and supported by appropriate evidence to underpin necessary findings.

Receipt of public funds will typically also turn on the question of whether, without an injection of public money, the project will proceed. If the project is a financially desirable project for a developer even in the absence of public funds, it is doubtful that public funds will be forthcoming.

The need to clean up existing environmental contamination is one condition that will often justify the use of public funds. The reasons for this we will discuss shortly.

I have a special interest in sustainable revitalization of environmentally challenged properties, including particularly the recycling and reuse of urban and suburban infill properties. I believe developers, business owners, and public officials should work together to meet the needs of urban and suburban communities through creation of revitalized downtowns, which offer a wide array of affordable, midpriced, and upscale housing and convenient retail shopping, dining, consumer service, health care, and entertainment options, as well as quality-of-life amenities.

Development and redevelopment of environmentally challenged property is referred to as *brownfield development*. The term *brownfield* is a descriptive term used to refer to environmentally challenged but still usable property.

Similarly, the term *greenfield development* refers to development of environmentally *clean* sites, typically comprised of undeveloped farmland. Some properties are so environmentally contaminated they cannot easily be restored to a usable condition. These properties are typically placed on a governmental list maintained my the United States Environmental Protection Agency, known as the National Priorities List, using the USEPA's Hazard Ranking System and are referred to as *superfund* sites. Brownfield sites, by definition, do not include superfund sites.

Brownfield development represents a prime opportunity. Brownfield sites, especially urban infill sites, are often in ideal locations for redevelopment. The public benefit of having these properties cleaned up may readily satisfy the public purpose test to qualify them for receipt of public money to aid in development.

In November 2006, the law establishing cleanup liability for environmentally contaminated property was significantly amended. This has resulted in a sea change in brownfield development opportunities. Prior to November 2006, the environmental strategy of developers and investors was to establish an *innocent purchaser* defense to cleanup liability. This required collection of evidence prior to acquisition to prove the acquiring party did not know a property was contaminated when acquired. Of course, the *innocent purchaser* defense was of little value in those circumstances where a party was acquiring a property known to be environmentally contaminated—*a brownfield.*

As of November 1, 2006, the law was amended to provide for an "exemption from cleanup liability" if a potentially responsible party can establish that any environmental contamination of a site already existed when the site was acquired and that the owner did not thereafter contribute additional contamination. This is done through what is referred to in the statute as an *all appropriate inquiry.*

The *all appropriate inquiry* standard is a legal standard, compliance with which should be confirmed by knowledgeable environmental counsel. If environmental cleanup litigation appears to be a significant risk, I often use Chicago attorney William J. Anaya to analyze the sufficiency of evidence gathered to evaluate my client's ability to establish in court that an *all appropriate inquiry* has, in fact, occurred. Bill is a seasoned environmental litigator particularly adept at evaluating the evidentiary value of environmental data gathered by environmental consultants. He understands the difference between litigation risks and transaction risks. Whoever you use for this purpose, be sure he or she understands that completing the transaction is the primary objective and that finding a way to quantify the risk of environmental cleanup liability is the outcome being sought. There are many so-called environmental lawyers and transaction lawyers who take the chicken-little approach by declaring *the sky is falling* rather than making a rational determination of actual exposure to liability. On the other hand, there are also a number of practitioners who do not fully understand that real financial risks from environmental contamination remain, notwithstanding the November 1, 2006, law change. If one does not understand the risks, it is not possible to effectively manage them.

Conducting an *all appropriate inquiry* requires a prospective purchaser to obtain a comprehensive environmental site assessment conducted by a qualified environmental professional using the appropriate analytic standard—currently the standard established by ASTM E1527-05. If an *all appropriate inquiry* is properly conducted, evidence will exist to establish the sought-after exemption from cleanup liability.

The great benefit of this new exemption from cleanup liability is that it removes a great risk factor previously associated with brownfield development—the risk of being required to pay for site cleanup. It is still the case that if a developer excavates contaminated soil, it must comply with environmental laws for handling special and hazardous waste and must dispose of it at a special waste site, but the previous risk of being forced to bear the potentially huge cost of cleaning up the site has been greatly reduced. Much environmental contamination can be dealt with by simply installing institutional controls, such as covering contaminated soil with asphalt or concrete parking lots or building slabs, which are already a necessary component of most development plans. This change in law has made the costs of brownfield development more readily quantifiable and controllable. Consequently, brownfield development has become less risky and more common.

Brownfield development presents an ideal opportunity for developers, local governments, and environmentalists to work together. It can represent the ultimate in recycling by restoring significant tracts of already environmentally contaminated land into safe, healthy, and productive development.

The development incentives described in this chapter for developing brownfields are, for the most part, available for commercial development in general, not just brownfield development. In any case where a municipality determines that a particular development will provide a desired public benefit to the community, the potential exists for obtaining governmental economic development incentives.

I use the brownfield development example in this chapter because I feel strongly that economic development of underused and abandoned properties found in many urban areas is vital to community revitalization. Brownfield development also represents, in many cases, the *easy case* for establishing public benefit sufficient to warrant use of public funds since most people accept the notion that returning environmentally contaminated property to productive use will, directly or indirectly, benefit the community as a whole.

Brownfield development has its own unique set of development issues, but as a general proposition, they can be adequately addressed if a way is found to offset and counterbalance the extra development costs and challenges they present.

Keep an open mind. Think outside the box. If your project obstacle is not environmental contamination but some other issue that will increase your cost of development, the approach to development and the economic incentives described in this chapter may very well work for you if you can demonstrate that the community at large will benefit as well.

Establishing a viable *public purpose* is not as easy at it may sound, but it is easier than you may think.

What follows is the case for using public money for private brownfield development, focusing on brownfield development in Illinois.

## Public Money for Private Brownfield Development

According to the Illinois Environmental Protection Agency (IEPA), it is difficult to determine the number of brownfields in the state of Illinois, but they are believed to exist in virtually every town and city. Brownfields consist of abandoned, unused, and underused commercial and industrial properties of almost every type. They include everything from abandoned gas stations to closed factories, warehouses, steel mills, and other properties that have ceased to be used to their highest and best use because of the presence or believed presence of environmental contamination.

These properties, referred to generally as *brownfields*, have not been redeveloped because of concerns regarding high cleanup costs, lengthy and complicated cleanup processes, potential liability risks, and active government involvement. These concerns have contributed to urban sprawl as developers have moved to develop untarnished *greenfields* on the outskirts of towns and cities. They have also contributed to urban blight as brownfields have been abandoned and left to decay, thereby resulting in reduced property values and deterioration of neighborhood communities, reduction in employment opportunities and tax revenue, potential harm to human health and the environment, vandalism, open dumping, and other illegal activity.

Revitalization of brownfields is an urgent concern in many communities. As a consequence, numerous programs and redevelopment incentives have been developed and implemented, and continue to be developed and implemented, to aid in the effort to return brownfields to productive use.

This chapter is focused primarily on the financial impact of environmental contamination on prospective brownfield redevelopment sites. Particularly, this chapter is focused on the availability of government funds to help pay costs associated with assessment and cleanup of brownfield sites to enable redevelopment into commercially productive projects.

Developers and development counsel are concerned with environmental issues but primarily because these issues may present obstacles to development or financing of a given project. Toxicity of environmental contamination, the regulatory scheme for permitting and regulation of activities presenting a recognized adverse environmental condition, and even the regulatory scheme for remediation of environmental conditions within a proposed development site are matters typically left to *environmental* lawyers and engineers. Developers and development counsel have other concerns.

Real estate development is driven by economics. Developers and development counsel dealing with brownfield properties are focused on four primary issues: (a) Will existing contamination interfere with the developer's intended use of the property? (b) What is the most cost-effective way to mitigate environmental concerns? (c) How will these costs impact the bottom-line economics of the intended project? (d) From what third-party sources are funds available to reduce or eliminate the economic impact of brownfield contamination on the developer's project development costs? The science and regulatory scheme pertinent to environmental contamination are left to others.

Understanding the development process is imperative to recognizing opportunities to obtain government money for private development. The development process will be discussed in detail later in this chapter.

The sources of government funds for brownfield redevelopment are varied. They fall into the broad category of what commercial real estate developers refer to as *entitlements*. While there are a few financial entitlements available to brownfield site developers, such as favorable tax treatment for brownfield site cleanup costs discussed below, the greatest opportunities to obtain government funds for brownfield site development are through the use of government incentive programs.

The main point to understand about government development incentives is that they are designed and intended primarily to benefit local government, not developers. This is not to say that they do not benefit developers. It is just to point out that benefiting developers is not their primary aim.

It is critical to understand this distinction when searching for government money to benefit private development. The way to obtain government money for private development is for the private developer to align its development plans with the needs of the public, as determined by local government.

If there is no public objective sought to be achieved by local government through development of a particular project, there will be no public money available for the project. Once again, availability of government funds for private development is an incentive, not a right. Developers are entitled to seek incentives, and if the developer fulfills the incentive's objective, it will be entitled to receive the benefits of the incentive program; but when it comes to receiving public money, use of the term *entitlement* is a nonsequitur. Use of public funds must primarily benefit the public. It is up to the developer to make sure its development plans coincide with the public good so that what benefits the public can benefit the developer as well.

Sometimes it is useful to meet with local public officials to educate them as to how the public will benefit from a particular project and why it is in the best interests of the public for local government to provide a development incentive to achieve that benefit.

It is also sometimes necessary to educate local public officials as to the sources of funds available to local governmental entities to provide development incentives to developers. Especially in smaller communities without a full-time economic development director or staff, local public officials may not be aware of the resources available to their community to stimulate local economic development.

Once public officials become convinced their public constituency will benefit from a project and can be shown how to receive those benefits with little or no out-of-pocket costs to local government, the stage is set. At this point, a development financing scenario that uses public funds for private development can be structured to the mutual benefit of the community at large and the private developer. Thus is born the so-called public-private partnership. It is not so much a partnership in fact as it is a mutual-benefit compact. It is a relationship that sets up the proverbial *win-win* scenario in which both the public sector and private sector benefit from private development through the use of public funds. This concept is the foundation for obtaining public money for private development.

# Public Funding Predicates

Before public money can be used for the benefit of a privately owned project, the project under consideration must satisfy the *public purpose test* established by the Fifth Amendment to the U.S. Constitution and many state constitutions.

In Illinois, for example, Article VIII, Section 1(a), of the Illinois Constitution sets forth the following requirement:

"Public funds, property or credit shall be used only for public purposes."

This constitutional requirement is known as the *public purpose test.*

The determination of what constitutes a *public purpose* has expanded over time. In *People ex rel. City of Salem v. McMackin,* 53 Ill. 2d 347, 291 N. E. 2d 807, 813 (1972), the petitioner challenged the constitutionality of the Industrial Project Revenue Bond Act based on the position that it violated the public purpose test because it allowed for the expenditure of public funds for a private purpose. The Illinois Supreme Court disagreed, finding that promotion of publicly desired economic development is a proper public purpose for the use of public funds, notwithstanding the fact that private entities may be the direct recipients of those public funds. The *McMackin* court held that

> if the principal purpose and objective in a given enactment is public in nature, it does not matter that there will be an incidental benefit to private interests . . . ."Public purpose" is not a static concept. It is flexible, and is capable of expansion to meet conditions of a complex society that were not within the contemplation of the framers of our constitution. (291 N.E.2d at 812-813)

Similarly, in *Clayton v. Village of Oak Park,* 117 Ill. App. 3d 560, 453 N. E. 2d 937, 943, 73 Ill. Dec. 112 (1st Dist. 1983), the court held that

> [w]hether a proposed expenditure serves public purposes is a determination initially made by the legislative body empowered to expend the resources . . . . Broad discretion is allowed in such matters . . . . There is no constitutional prohibition against the use of public funds which inure to the benefit of private interests, provided that the money is employed for a public purpose. (Citations omitted)

See also *People ex rel. City of Urbana v. Paley,* 68 Ill. 2d 62, 368 N. E. 2d 915, 920-921, 11 Ill. Dec. 307 (1977). ("[T]he application of the public-purpose doctrine to sanction urban redevelopment can no longer be restricted to areas where crime, vacancy, or physical decay produce undesirable living conditions or imperil public health. Stimulation of commercial growth and removal of economic stagnation are also objectives which enhance the public weal.")

Similarly, the issue of whether economic development constitutes a sufficient *public purpose* was the threshold issue determined by the U.S. Supreme Court in *Kelo v. City of New London, Connecticut,* 545 U.S. 469, 162 L. Ed. 2d 439, 125 S. Ct. 2655 (2005). Although *Kelo* involved an eminent domain proceeding under the Takings Clause of the Fifth Amendment to the U.S. Constitution, the challenge to its validity was whether a sufficient public purpose was served by the city of New London's proposed economic development plan to authorize governmental taking of the Kelo property for transfer and redevelopment by another private party. The U.S. Supreme Court affirmed that it was, stating,

> The City [of New London] has carefully formulated an economic development plan that it believes will provide appreciable benefits to the community, including—but by no

means limited to—new jobs and increased tax revenue. As with other exercises in urban planning and development, the City is endeavoring to coordinate a variety of commercial, residential, and recreational uses of land, with the hope that they will form a whole greater than the sum of its parts. To effectuate this plan, the City has invoked a state statute that specifically authorizes the use of eminent domain to promote economic development. Given the comprehensive character of the plan, the thorough deliberation that preceded its adoption, and the limited scope of our review, it is appropriate for us . . . to resolve the challenges of the individual owners, not on a piecemeal basis, but rather in light of the entire plan. Because the plan unquestionably serves a public purpose, the takings challenged here satisfy the public use requirement of the Fifth Amendment . . . . Promoting economic development is a traditional and long accepted function of government. There is, moreover, no principled way of distinguishing economic development from the other public purposes that we have recognized. (125 S.Ct. at 2665)

## The "But-for" Test

In applying the public purpose test to economic development incentives benefiting private entities, the but-for test is generally applied by asking the following question: but for the granting of the economic incentive, would the economic development desired by the municipality occur? If the answer is no, then the use of public funds as an incentive for the targeted development is a proper public purpose.

There is no specific statutory or constitutional provision in Illinois specifying a but-for analysis to the granting of economic incentives must be used, but it is widely accepted that the but-for test is the correct analytic approach. An example of this analysis for purposes of economic incentives under the Tax Increment Allocation Redevelopment Act (TIF

Act), 65 ILCS 5/11-74.4-1, et seq., is set forth in *Castel Properties, Ltd. v. City of Marion,* 259 Ill. App. 3d 432, 631 N. E. 2d 459, 465, 197 Ill. Dec. 456 (5th Dist. 1994). Even if a but-for test is not a legally mandated test for all economic incentives using pubic funds (as is occasionally argued), from a practical standpoint, it will likely be a necessary part of convincing a municipality that an economic incentive in the form of public funds should be granted.

Remember that public economic development assistance programs are intended as *incentives* to entice private development to achieve a public good. The programs are not designed to primarily benefit private developers. Accordingly, to receive public funds for a private project, a developer will ordinarily need to demonstrate that (1) the project benefits the public good, and (2) "but for" the commitment of public funds, the project will not go forward—at least not in a way that achieves the maximum benefit to the public sought by local public officials.

## Satisfying Public Funding Predicates

As fundamental as the public purpose test and the but-for test are as predicates to receiving public money for private development, they are not as difficult to satisfy as one might imagine.

Real estate development is an intensely local undertaking. Competition exists within and between local communities to attract development. Commercial real estate development, particularly retail development, can be a great benefit to local governments because it enhances the real estate tax base and increases sales tax revenue. Real estate tax revenue and sales tax revenue are the two primary sources of revenue available to local governments to pay for governmental services.

The benefits to local governments to be obtained by offering incentives for developers to clean up and redevelop brownfield sites within the community are numerous. They are recognized to include revitalization of blighted and decaying areas, decreased pollution, increased jobs, expanded retail choices for local residents, relief of the tax burden on local residents, increased value in the tax base (enabling increased spending on city services and education and improving the quality of life for all residents through the creation of public amenities, such as parks and open space, creating a generally more satisfying living environment). These are all proper objectives for local government. Public funds may properly be spent by local governments to obtain these benefits. *McMackin, supra,* 291 N. E. 2d at 812.

Brownfield development incentives, like all government development incentives, are just that—incentives. They are designed and intended to induce developers to build the types of development within a community that local governments believe are needed to benefit local residents. Development incentives are bargaining chips, so to speak. They are the currency in trade to *purchase* the kinds of development local government seeks.

Virtually all brownfield development programs and other development programs enacted or created by state and federal governments are designed to provide a source of funds to be used by municipalities and other units of local government to entice developers to build the types of developments local public officials determine they need. Government funds may not be available in every case, but when government funds are available, commercial real estate projects that would not otherwise be economically feasible can be made profitable.

To understand the full scope of government funds available for private development of brownfield sites, it is first necessary to understand some basic concepts applicable to commercial real estate development in general. Without this understanding, valuable opportunities for seeking and obtaining government funds for brownfield development, including environmental investigation and remediation, will be lost.

# The Development Process

All commercial real estate developments involve four primary areas of concern. These four aspects of commercial real estate development are the primary focus of every real estate development and redevelopment project:

1. market demand,
2. access,
3. use, and
4. finances.

These aspects of commercial real estate development were discussed in chapter 7, "'It Ain't Rocket Science,' but . . ."

The issue of brownfield site development implicates the *use* and *finances* aspects of commercial real estate development.

The presence of certain hazardous substances, pollutants, or contaminants may impair the ability of a site to be used as intended by a developer absent remediation to remove environmentally offensive substances or, where applicable, installation of suitable institutional controls to limit their exposure.

Developers and development counsel may not be versed in the technical aspects of toxicity of regulated substances that may contaminate a potential development site. What they do know is that the presence of these substances in quantities that require cleanup or installation of institutional controls adds costs to real estate projects that would not be incurred if these substances were not present.

From a developer's standpoint, these costs are *extras*. Environmental cleanup and installation of institutional controls add to the cost of site development but do not add to its value. If $1 million in extra cost is incurred to investigate and clean up a brownfield site to build a two-hundred-thousand-leasable-square-foot shopping center, but the same two-hundred-thousand-leasable-square-foot project could be built across the street on a *clean* site, the developer developing the brownfield site will be at a competitive disadvantage to another developer who develops the clean site. If the going rental rate for retail space is $40 per square foot in the geographic area in which the two sites are located, it is not likely that prospective tenants will be willing to pay more rental per square foot simply because the brownfield site developer paid more to develop its project. As a consequence, the brownfield site developer's return on investment will be less because—all else being equal—it has $1 million more invested in the project than does the developer of the clean site across the street.

This fundamental financial reality becomes particularly significant when the street separating the brownfield site and the clean site is a city or village boundary, with one site in one municipality and the other in another municipality. This is especially true if, in fact, market demand will support development of only one of the two sites with the hypothetical two-hundred-thousand-leasable-square-foot shopping center so that competition exists between two municipalities to get the project built within one of their municipal boundaries.

Why would local government officials care if the site is built within their community instead of the one next door? Because municipalities primarily rely on real estate tax revenue and sales tax revenue to pay the costs of running the municipality and to pay for municipal government services like police and fire protection, street maintenance, snow removal, and the like. If the project is built in their municipality, it will enjoy the benefits of increased real estate taxes and sales taxes the project brings with it. If it is built across the street in another municipality, it will not.

Even when intermunicipal competition for tax dollars is not an issue, development of brownfield sites is desirable to municipalities because it can change the character of the property from a blighted, unhealthy eyesore to a productive, tax-generating enterprise. This change can increase the taxable value of not only the brownfield site but also the surrounding properties, as well as create jobs and serve as a catalyst for urban renewal.

The key point is that there is a recognized public interest in returning brownfield sites to productive use. Understanding this can open the door to governmental support for brownfield site redevelopment.

Where some miss the boat in reviewing brownfield site reimbursement programs is their assumption that if the eligible recipient for reimbursement is a *municipality*, the program does nothing to help a developer. From the commercial real estate developer's perspective, the precise method for eliminating the *extra* costs associated with brownfield site redevelopment is not the point. The point is that the developer avoids incurring these costs, or that a suitable method is provided for the developer to recover these costs, so that the developer's ability to finance the project is not impaired and the developer is able to receive its required rate of return on investment.

Whether looking at *direct benefits* or *indirect benefits* to commercial real estate developers, there are a number of opportunities available in Illinois, and in most other states, for private developers to receive the benefits of government money to make their real estate projects profitable. For a commercial real estate developer, this is *found money*. If developers overlook available opportunities to have government funds help pay for brownfield site redevelopment costs, they will miss valuable development opportunities and find themselves at a competitive disadvantage to their competitors.

Because of the recognized social value in redeveloping urban brownfield sites, existing financial assistance programs are being extended, and new financial assistance programs are being put in place.

# Sources of Government Funds to Benefit Private Development

When exploring available government funds to help pay for assessment and cleanup of brownfield sites, there are two avenues of approach. The first is to consider programs specifically designed to facilitate brownfield site redevelopment. The other is to consider more generalized sources of government assistance to developers that, while not designed primarily for use in brownfield redevelopment, are nonetheless available for this purpose in the proper case.

The problem with brownfield-specific programs is that they are often subject to inconsistent funding by state and federal governments. It is not unusual for brownfield-specific programs to be enacted into law then left unfunded. Non-brownfield-specific economic development programs are less likely to suffer this fate. Still, when funded, brownfield-specific programs are a valuable tool to facilitate payment of expenses related to brownfield assessment and cleanup so that redevelopment can take place.

## Brownfield-Specific Programs

On January 11, 2002, the Small Business Liability Relief and Brownfields Revitalization Act (Brownfields Act), Pub. L. No. 107-118, 115 Stat. 2356, was signed into law. The specific purpose of the act was

> [t]o provide certain relief for small businesses from liability under the Comprehensive Environmental Response, Compensation, and Liability Act of 1980, and to amend such Act to promote the cleanup and reuse of brownfields, to provide financial assistance for brownfields revitalization, to enhance State response programs, and for other purposes.

It should be noted that the Brownfields Act is actually two acts combined into one. Title I is the Small Business Liability Protection Act, and Title II is the Brownfields Revitalization and Environmental Restoration Act of 2001. Each amends the Comprehensive Environmental Response, Compensation, and Liability Act of 1980 (CERCLA), 42 USC Section 9601 et seq.

Largely ignored by much of the environmental bar is Title II, Subtitle A, entitled "Brownfields Revitalization Funding," which amended CERCLA Section 101, 42 USC Section 9601, by adding at the end a definition of *brownfield site*. See 42 USC Section 9601(39).

Title II, Subtitle A, also amended CERCLA Section 104 to establish a program to provide grants to "eligible entities to provide assistance for the remediation of brownfield sites [among other uses] in the form of . . . loans to an eligible entity, a site owner, a site developer, or another person" (42 USC Section 9604[k][3]). It also provides that an eligible entity may in some cases provide assistance for remediation of brownfield sites in the form of one or more grants. *Id.*

A *brownfield site* is defined specifically, for purposes of federal law, by CERCLA at 42 USC Section 9601(39). It is a lengthy definition that, generally summarized, includes most sites impacted by adverse environmental concerns but, most notably, excludes superfund sites.

For purposes of this book, I will forgo a detailed legal analysis of brownfield-specific funding programs. While this chapter is focused on brownfield development, my objective in this book is to expose you to more generalized development incentives that may be available not only to brownfields development, but to economic development incentives available for a wide range of real estate development. Although this chapter, by necessity, includes a lot of *law*, this book is not a book written primarily for lawyers.

The economic development incentives described in this chapter are available for both brownfield development and nonbrownfield development, assuming you can fulfill the public purpose test. As the U.S. Supreme Court in *Kelo vs. City of New London*, infra, made clear, the need to stimulate general economic development, by itself, can be a legitimate public purpose to justify use of public funds.

For my lawyer friends, a detailed analysis of brownfield-specific programs can be found in the Illinois Institute for Continuing Legal Education (IICLE) handbook published in 2007, titled *Environmental Law in Illinois Corporate and Real Estate Transactions*. My chapter on this subject is handbook chapter 8, titled "Brownfield Development: Public Money for Private Development." Please contact IICLE directly to acquire a copy of the handbook by visiting the IICLE Web site at *www.iicle.com*.

## Non-Brownfield-Specific Redevelopment Programs

There are many public funding initiatives for commercial real estate development that can be used for a wide array of economic development projects, far beyond projects involving brownfields and brownfield development.

Some key non-brownfield-specific economic development programs, such as tax increment financing (TIF) and business district development financing, have the added advantage of being essentially *self-funding*. As such, they escape the sometimes-fickle funding priorities of state and federal governments.

Finding funding sources for brownfield development projects beyond the incentive programs specifically limited to brownfield redevelopment requires a fair amount of thinking outside the box. To do this, it is useful to step away from the narrow focus of *brownfield redevelopment programs* and look at the broader scope of government programs designed to provide redevelopment incentives in general.

## General Economic Development Incentives

All government development incentive programs are designed to close the financial gap that stands as a barrier to free market development. Private sector real estate development is driven primarily by economics. Developers require a profit commensurate with the capital demands and the economic risks the project presents. Investors require an acceptable rate of return on investment and have a wide array of alternative investment opportunities to achieve their required investment yield if a particular real estate project fails to provide an adequate yield.

With this reality in mind, one can begin to understand that the precise nature of the economic barrier is less important than recognition that all economic barriers must be overcome. Brownfields are more expensive to redevelop than land or buildings not having environmental contamination. The fact that they cost more to redevelop does not increase their intrinsic economic value. Any government incentive program designed as a financial incentive to encourage development can be a viable source of funds for brownfield redevelopment if it helps close the financial gap.

Recognizing that brownfields are often located in aging, blighted, or underdeveloped areas municipalities may wish to revitalize, attention should be focused on economic development incentives that may aid brownfield redevelopment even when that is not their stated primary purpose. The corollary to that observation is that there are a wide variety of economic development programs designed to promote development and redevelopment of aging, blighted, and underdeveloped areas of cities and towns whether or not they are burdened with major environmental concerns.

Home rule communities in Illinois, in particular, have a virtually limitless ability to provide economic assistance to developers provided the *public use test* can be satisfied and provided the municipality believes the economic development assistance is in the best interests of the community.

## Tax Abatement and Rebate Programs in Illinois

A variety of statutory provisions have been enacted in Illinois to permit home rule and non-home rule units of government to abate and rebate taxes within limits defined by statute. Some of these are highlighted below and are representative of the kind of development incentives available in many other states. Illinois is not unique in its efforts to promote economic development within its borders.

The Illinois constitution establishes *home rule* for qualifying communities that make them largely autonomous units of government with broad powers to tax and control their own economic destiny. Non-home rule communities are subject to much greater control by the state. Non-home rule municipalities may abate or rebate taxes only within limits specifically authorized by statute. For home rule units of government, authority to abate and rebate taxes is not limited by statutory pronouncements of the state legislature.

Article VII, Section 6(a), of the Illinois Constitution provides that "[e]xcept as limited by this Section, a home rule unit may exercise any power and perform any function pertaining to its government and affairs including, but not limited to . . . tax."

This constitutional power has been construed broadly to include, among other powers, the power of Illinois home rule units of government to grant real estate tax abatements, sales tax rebates, and exemptions to real estate transfer taxes "unless restricted by a constitutional provision or appropriate legislation." See *Stahl v. Village of Hoffman Estates*, 296 Ill. App. 3d 550,

143

694 N. E. 2d 1102, 1105, 230 Ill. Dec. 824 (1st Dist. 1998). Absent a constitutional or statutory restriction, home rule units of government have virtually unlimited power to tax and to abate or rebate taxes so long as such power is exercised in furtherance of a proper public purpose, including the facilitation of private economic development that local governmental officials have determined will benefit the community at large. *People ex rel. City of Salem v. McMackin,* 53 Ill. 2d 347, 291 N. E. 2d 807 (1972); *Clayton v. Village of Oak Park,* 117 Ill. App. 3d 560, 453 N. E. 2d 937, 73 Ill. Dec. 112 (1st Dist. 1983); *Kelo v. City of New London, Connecticut,* 545 U.S. 469, 162 L. Ed. 2d 439, 125 S. Ct. 2655 (2005).

In Illinois, for retail shopping center developments in particular, sales tax rebate agreements between municipalities and private developers have become a particularly popular and useful device for enabling developers to recoup the extra costs incurred to rehabilitate and redevelop brownfield projects. The case can easily and clearly be made that, absent redevelopment into a retail use, an abandoned brownfield would generate no sales tax revenue. Inducing redevelopment by allocating to the developer, by amount or for a specified period, part or all the sales tax revenue generated upon redevelopment creates a *win-win* arrangement for the municipality and the developer. The developer is able to recover the extraordinary costs incurred in developing the brownfield site, and the municipality gets the benefit of needed development, including an increased real estate tax base and future sales tax revenue.

## Tax Increment Financing (TIF) in Illinois

One of the most widely used redevelopment financing tools to promote community economic development is tax increment financing (TIF). This tool is available in various forms in most of the United States. In Illinois, for example, it is authorized by the Tax Increment Allocation Redevelopment Act (TIF Act), 65 ILCS 5/11-74.4-1 et seq. Under the TIF Act, incremental tax revenues derived from the tax rates of various taxing districts in a redevelopment project area may be used for the payment of eligible redevelopment project costs incurred to redevelop a *blighted area* or *conservation area*, as each of these terms is defined in the TIF Act 65 ILCS 5/11-74.4-3(a), 5/11-74.4-3(b).

The TIF Act, including particularly its requirements for establishing that a proposed redevelopment project area qualifies as a blighted area or conservation area, is complex and demanding. A complete analysis of the procedure for qualifying an area as blighted, creating a TIF redevelopment project area, and determining all qualifying expenses that may be recovered is beyond the scope of this chapter. For an in-depth discussion of the Illinois TIF Act and its requirements, refer to *Municipal Law Series Volume 3: Financing, Tax, and Municipal Property*, chapter 6 (IICLE, 2006), available at *www.iicle.com*. Similar publications likely exist within your own jurisdiction.

As a general matter, however, it is often the case that brownfields fall within the areas qualified as blighted areas or conservation areas under the TIF Act.

Many municipalities have in place existing redevelopment project areas (TIF districts) for which applications may be made to receive reimbursement for eligible redevelopment project costs from available tax increment revenue that may not have been previously fully allocated. Useful information concerning existing TIF districts and the availability of unallocated TIF funds often can be obtained by contacting the local TIF administrator, economic development staff, or local village planner.

In areas not already subject to an existing TIF district, a brownfield developer may wish to make the case for establishment of a *redevelopment project area* (TIF district) to offset eligible redevelopment project costs for a brownfield redevelopment project to the extent such redevelopment project costs stand as a barrier to development. Once again, such costs and financial assistance may qualify as an appropriate use of public funds and may be made available if, in their absence, the project will not be built.

Once again using the Illinois TIF Act as an example, the following definitions are particularly relevant for determining the potential for TIF financing for a brownfield project:

a.  *Redevelopment project* is defined as "any public or private development project in furtherance of the objectives of a redevelopment plan" (65 ILCS 5/11-74.4-3[*o*]).

b.  *Redevelopment project area* is defined as "an area designated by the municipality, which is not less in the aggregate than one and one-half acres and in respect to which the municipality has made a finding that there exist conditions which cause the area to be classified as an industrial park conservation area or a blighted area or a conservation area, or a combination of both blighted areas and conservation areas" 65 (ILCS 5/11-74.4-3[p]). (The definition of *industrial park conservation area* is found at 65 ILCS 5/11-74.4-3[c].)

c.  *Redevelopment project costs* means "and include[s] the sum total of all reasonable or necessary costs incurred or estimated to be incurred, and any such costs incidental to the redevelopment plan and redevelopment project" (65 ILCS 5/11-74.4-3[q]). Redevelopment project costs include, without limitation, the following:

1.  "[c]osts of studies, surveys, development of plans, and specifications, implementation and administration of the redevelopment plan including but not limited to staff and professional service costs for architectural, *engineering, legal, financial,* planning or other services" [emphasis added] (65 ILCS 5/11-74.4-3(q)(1));

2.  property assembly costs, "including but not limited to acquisition of land and other property, real or personal,

or rights or interests therein, demolition of buildings, site preparation, *site improvements that serve as an engineered barrier addressing ground level or below ground level environmental contamination*, including, but not limited to parking lots and other concrete or asphalt barriers, and the clearing and grading of land" (65 ILCS 5/11-74.4-3[q][2]; emphasis added);

3. costs of rehabilitation, "reconstruction or repair or remodeling of existing public or private buildings [but not construction of new buildings except public buildings demolished to enable use of the site for private investment or to permit the site to be devoted to a different use requiring private investment], fixtures, and leasehold improvements" (65 ILCS 5/11-74.4-3[q][3]);

4. costs of construction of certain public works as limited by statute (65 ILCS 5/11-74.4-3[q][4]);

5. costs of job training and retraining projects, "including the cost of 'welfare to work' programs implemented by businesses located within the redevelopment project area" (65 ILCS 5/11-74.4-3[q][5]);

6. financing costs, "including but not limited to all necessary and incidental expenses relating to the issuance of obligations and which may include payment of interest on any obligations issued . . . including interest accruing during the estimated period of construction of any redevelopment project for which such obligations are issued and for not exceeding 36 months thereafter and including reasonable reserves related thereto" (65 ILCS 5/11-74.4-3[q][6]); and

7. various other costs eligible as *redevelopment project costs* that may be paid from TIF proceeds (65 ILCS 5/11-74.4-3[q][7]-5/11-74.4-3[q][13]).

An important *exclusion* from the definition of eligible *redevelopment project costs* is set forth at 65 ILCS 5/11-74.4-3(q)(12), which provides, "Unless explicitly stated herein the cost of construction of new privately-owned buildings shall not be an eligible redevelopment project cost."

Another useful attribute of TIF financing is that instead of TIF proceeds being paid to the developer over time, *as collected*, a municipality may agree to sell TIF bonds to be paid off with the TIF income stream. In such case, the developer may receive payment of eligible redevelopment project costs as incurred. From a practical standpoint, it is usually easier to get a municipality to pay the developer TIF proceeds on an as-collected basis rather than take the risk that TIF proceeds will be insufficient to pay off TIF bonds. However, if the municipality is adequately benefited and the project will not proceed otherwise, the municipality does have the power to sell bonds to permit up-front funding. The chances for TIF bond financing increase if the developer arranges for the purchase of the bonds when issued by finding a bond purchaser (which may include the developer, who may then hold or resell the bonds).

## Business District Development and Redevelopment in Illinois

Effective January 1, 2005, Illinois Municipal Code Section 11-74.3-1 et seq., titled "Business District Development and Redevelopment," 65 ILCS 5/11-74.3-1 et seq., was substantially amended by PA 93-1053 to grant new development and redevelopment powers to Illinois municipalities. In many respects, these provisions are similar to the TIF Act discussed in Section 8.42 above; but they have a different revenue-raising mechanism and, in many respects, are easier to work with than the TIF Act.

Pursuant to the business district development statutes, a municipality may designate an area of the municipality as a *business district* (65 ILCS 5/11-74.3-2). Once an area is designated as a business district, the municipality has broad powers to carry out a business district development or redevelopment plan (65 ILCS 5/11-74.3-3).

Among the powers granted to municipalities is the power

12. [t]o impose a retailers' occupation tax [sales tax] and a service occupation tax in the business district for the planning, execution, and implementation of business district plans and to pay for business district project costs as set forth in the business district plan approved by the municipality;

13. [t]o impose a hotel operators' occupation tax in the business district for the planning, execution, and implementation of business district plans and to pay for the business district project costs as set forth in the business district plan approved by the municipality;

14. [t]o issue obligations in one or more series bearing interest at rates determined by the corporate authorities of the municipality by ordinance and secured by the business district tax allocation fund set forth in Section 11-74.3-6 for the business district to provide for the payment of business district project costs. (65 ILCS 5/11-74.3-3[12] through 5/11-74.3-3[14])

The business district tax imposed pursuant to 65 ILCS 5/11-74.3-3(12) and 5/11-74.3-3(13) may be imposed in .25% increments, up to a maximum tax of 1% (65 ILCS 5/11-74.3-6[b], 5/11-74.3-6[d]). The tax applies only within the designated business district and may remain in effect until all business district project costs and all municipal obligations financing the business district project costs, if any, have been paid in accordance with the business district development or redevelopment plan, but in no event longer than twenty-three years after the date the plan was adopted by ordinance (65 ILCS 5/11-74.3-6[a]).

The taxing authority granted by 65 ILCS 5/11-74.3-2 through 5/11-74.3-4 is available to both non-home rule municipalities and home rule municipalities.

The term *business district project costs* is not defined in the statute except by reference to the qualification that they must be "set forth in the business district plan approved by the municipality" (65 ILCS 5/11-74.3-3[12], 5/11-74.3-3[13]).

The Business District Development and Redevelopment Act declares at 65 ILCS 5/11-74.3-1(3) that the exercise of powers granted therein to develop or redevelop business districts constitutes "a public use essential to the public interest." As such, it would appear that any project costs set forth in the business district plan approved by the municipality should satisfy the public purpose test. Certainly, since remediation of environmental contamination is widely accepted to be in the interest of public health and safety, any project costs approved by the municipality in its business district plan for payment of brownfield remediation expenses also appear to satisfy the public purpose test.

Creation of business districts under the business district development and redevelopment statutes appears to be a much less demanding process than the sometimes cumbersome process of establishing blight as a predicate to using the TIF Act. This advantage has been called into question, however, by a recent decision by the Illinois Appellate Court, Fifth District, filed on July 3, 2008, in Docket No. 5-07-0142 titled *Randy Geisler et al. v. the City of Wood River, Illinois et al.*

In the *Wood River* case, the Fifth District Appellate Court concluded, at pages 18-23 of the opinion, that if a business district development plan involves an agreement of the municipality to share retailer occupation taxes (sales taxes) collected pursuant to 6z-18 of the State Finance Act, the business district statute must be read and interpreted together with Section 8-11-20 of the Illinois Municipal Code, requiring specific findings of blight.

It has been noted that the city of Wood River, Illinois, is not a home rule unit of government. It should also be noted, however, that Section 8-11-20(b) of the Illinois Municipal Code expressly makes home rule units of government subject to the requirements of Section 8-11-20(a), the interpretation of which was the subject of the *Wood River* case.

If the decision is upheld, one of the widely perceived advantages of creating a business district instead of a TIF district is diminished. If a specific finding of blight is required to enter into a revenue sharing agreement between a municipality and a private developer, consideration must be given to whether the additional funding opportunities available under the TIF statute make it the preferable choice.

Still, the business district development and redevelopment statutes have some key attributes that may still make establishment of a business district desirable.

Since the incremental taxes generated pursuant to 65 ILCS 5/11-74.3-3(12) and 5/11-74.3-3(13) are in addition to any other tax and are essentially *convenience taxes* paid by consumers actually receiving the benefit of business services located in the business district, the net cost to the municipality is virtually zero. With rising transportation and fuel costs, the *convenience* benefit may likewise become a direct economic benefit to nearby shoppers.

This attribute may be particularly useful where there is a positive imbalance between sales taxes applicable to purchases in the business district compared with sales taxes applicable in other nearby retail centers.

For instance, sales taxes applicable to purchases from stores located in Cook County, Illinois, are among the highest in the nation. Sales taxes applicable in the collar counties surrounding Cook County, Illinois, are several percentage points less. There is much anecdotal evidence that shoppers from Cook County, Illinois, are prone to shop in neighboring counties to avoid paying 3% to 4% higher sales taxes applicable in Cook County. Even if a business district in a neighboring county were to add a full 1% sales tax within the business district, consumers can reasonably be expected to choose to shop at stores in that business district rather than pay still higher sales taxes applicable to stores in nearby Cook County. Conversely, use of a business district in Cook County may have the opposite affect since any increase in sales taxes would create an even more negative imbalance in applicable sales taxes from what already exists.

In the proper setting, the business district development and redevelopment statute represents a powerful tool for use by municipalities to pay for brownfield redevelopment and to reimburse developers for extraordinary project costs associated with brownfield redevelopment within an established business district.

## Real Estate Tax Abatement in Illinois

a. *Home Rule Authority*

As described above, home rule municipalities in Illinois have expansive power to abate and rebate taxes pursuant to authority granted under Article VII, Section 6(b), of the Illinois Constitution. Still, under most circumstances, home rule authority to abate taxes is limited to abatement of taxes levied only by the home rule municipality.

Section 18-180 of the Property Tax Code, 35 ILCS 200/18-180, extends the authority of home rule municipalities to abate all real estate taxes against qualifying properties located in areas of urban decay, within the limitations set forth therein. The authority granted to home rule municipalities is unique in that under specified circumstances, the home rule municipality has comprehensive authority to abate all real estate taxes levied against a qualified property, including taxes levied by other taxing districts. Qualified properties are limited to residential properties located in areas of urban decay. Areas of urban decay often include a concentration of brownfield sites, making this provision potentially useful as a brownfield redevelopment incentive that includes residential dwellings.

The Property Tax Code limits the total abatement for any tax year to "2% of the taxes extended by all taxing districts on all parcels located within the township that contain residential dwelling units of 6 units or less" (35 ILCS 18-180[a]). The abatement may extend a maximum of ten years and, in the final four years of the abatement period, must be reduced by 20% per year (35 ILCS 18-180[c]).

*b. Non-Home Rule Authority*

Non-home rule municipalities in Illinois are subject to much greater limitations of their authority to abate and rebate real estate taxes. Still, non-home rule municipalities do have statutory authority to abate real estate taxes in some circumstances for the purpose of encouraging commercial and industrial development (35 ILCS 200/18-165[a][1]). When seeking tax abatements for redevelopment of brownfields in non-home rule communities, the scope and limitations of 35 ILCS 100/18-165(a)(1) should be examined.

## Tax Abatements in Cook County, Illinois

Counties and municipalities often work together to provide real estate tax abatements to promote desired economic development within their boundaries. Cook County, Illinois, has adopted a variety of property tax incentives illustrative of how this type of incentive program may be set up.

Cook County, Illinois, for example, divides property tax incentives by property class. Of particular interest are class 6b, industrial development;

class 6c, environmental cleanup and development; class 7a and 7b, commercial development; class 8, industrial or commercial development; class 9, multifamily residential development; and class L, industrial or commercial development.

Under each one of these tax incentive programs, a real estate tax reduction of up to 50% of property taxes is available for a term of twelve years (except for class 9, which is for only ten years). In some cases, the tax reduction is renewable at the end of the applicable term for an additional period of time.

A detailed outline of tax incentive programs available in Cook County, Illinois, to promote economic development can be accessed through the Economic Development Resource Guide found at *www.enterpriz. org/edrg/cc.asp*.

## Federal Historic Preservation Tax Incentives

Another valuable tool to finance brownfield redevelopment costs can sometimes be found in the Federal Historic Preservation Tax Incentives Program. It is not uncommon for older buildings, some with genuine historic significance, to be burdened by environmental conditions that may substantially add to costs of renovation and rehabilitation. These conditions may come from large amounts of asbestos-containing materials, lead pipes, lead-based paint, petroleum spills, and other environmentally undesirable materials. Often, historic buildings in need of rehabilitation are in urban areas that have become blighted and are in desperate need of revitalization.

The Federal Historic Preservation Tax Incentives Program was created to provide economic assistance to developers seeking to save historic buildings and to encourage reuse of old structures. The program is administered by the National Park Service (NPS) and the IRS. See 36 CFR pt. 67 and visit *www.nps.gov/history/hps/tps/tax*.

There are two incentive regimes under this program: one to assist with the restoration of historic buildings and the other to assist with restoration of nonhistoric buildings built before 1936. A greater tax incentive is granted for historic buildings than nonhistoric buildings, but the incentives for each type of building are valuable.

   *a.   Historic Building 20% Tax Credit*

Under the Federal Historic Preservation Tax Incentives Program, a property may be entitled to a 20% federal income tax credit if the property is certified by the National Park Service (NPS) as a *certified historic structure* and is rehabilitated for commercial, industrial, agricultural, or rental residential purposes. As a *tax credit*, this incentive represents a dollar-for-dollar reduction in taxes.

A *certified historic structure* is a building (1) listed on the Lists of National Historic Landmarks (*www.nps.gov/history/nhl/designations/listsofnhls. htm*), (2) listed individually on the National Register of Historic Places (*www.nps.gov/nr*), or (3) located in a registered historic district and certified by the NPS as contributing to the district's historic significance. Detailed information on certification is available at *www.cr.nps.gov/hps/ tps/tax/hpcappl.htm*.

To be entitled to the 20% historic preservation tax credit, the NPS must (1) certify that a proposed rehabilitation of a certified historic structure is consistent with the historic character of the property, (2) approve the work before and during the work process, and (3) certify that the project meets the standards of rehabilitation specified by the NPS.

Also, the rehabilitation project must satisfy the following criteria established by the IRS: (1) the building is depreciable, (2) the rehabilitation is substantial (expenditures in excess of $5,000), (3) the property must be returned to active use, and (4) the building must be a certified historic structure at the time it is returned to active use.

The 20% tax credit is claimed in the year the rehabilitated property is placed back in service. The building owner must hold the building for a minimum of five years after completing the rehabilitation work or risk tax credit recapture.

### b. Nonhistoric Building 10% Tax Credit

Preservation tax credits are not limited to certified historic buildings. A 10% federal income tax credit is available for renovation of nonhistoric buildings built prior to 1936 that are rehabilitated for nonresidential use. This tax credit may be particularly useful for redevelopment of a vast number of brownfield sites, including former factories, warehouses, and manufacturing facilities containing environmental contamination or located on environmentally contaminated sites.

To qualify for the 10% nonhistoric building tax credit, the following criteria must be met: (1) the building must have been built prior to 1936, (2) at least 50% of the building's exterior walls existing at the time the renovation begins must remain in place as external walls when the project is complete, (3) at least 75% of the building's exterior walls existing at the time the renovation begins must remain in place as either external or internal walls when the project is complete, and (4) at least 75% of the building's internal structural framework existing at the time the renovation begins must remain in place when the project is complete.

Additional information about this tax credit is available at *www.nps. gov/history/hps/tps/tax/brochure1.htm#10.*

*c. Provisions Applicable to Both Historic and Nonhistoric Preservation Tax Credits*

The historic preservation tax incentives may be combined with other redevelopment incentives available to brownfield redevelopment, such as low-income housing tax credits.

Historic preservation tax incentives are assignable and can be sold and transferred to others to raise funds for the redevelopment project to pay for brownfield assessment and cleanup or other redevelopment project costs.

*d. Contact Information*

More information about historic preservation tax incentives is available through the National Park Service as follows:

> National Park Service
> Federal Historic Preservation Tax Incentives
> Heritage Preservation Services
> 1201 "Eye" St. NW (2255)
> Washington DC 20005
> 202-513-7270
> Web inquiries: *NPS_Hps-info@nps.gov*
> *www.cr.nps.gov/hps/tps/tax*

In Illinois, applications for certification of a structure as a *certified historic structure* are generally filed first with the Illinois State Historic Preservation Agency. The point of contact for Federal Historic Preservation Tax Incentives is generally the State Historic Preservation officer. Information concerning preservation projects and qualification for Federal

Historic Preservation Tax Incentives can be obtained through the Illinois Historic Preservation Agency:

> Illinois Historic Preservation Agency
> Preservation Services
> #1 Old State Capitol Plaza
> Springfield IL 62701-1507
> 217-782-4836

Instructions for completing the historic preservation certification application are available at *www.state.il.us/hpa/ps/taxcreditap.htm*.

## Low-Income Housing Tax Credits (LIHTC)—Federal

Because brownfields contribute to urban blight and reduce property values, there is often a direct relationship between the presence of brownfields in a community and a prevalence of low-income families. A concentration of low-income families and the high cost of redeveloping brownfields combine to create a disincentive for developers to revitalize blighted and distressed communities.

A shortage of quality, affordable housing is a particular concern in these communities and was the impetus for creation of the Low-Income Housing Tax Credit (LIHTC) Program. The LIHTC Program was created under the Tax Reform Act of 1986 and is codified at Section 42 of the Internal Revenue Code.

LIHTCs can provide investors and developers of eligible affordable housing with a huge tax savings. As tax credits, LIHTCs represent a dollar-for-dollar reduction in federal income taxes. All LIHTCs are taken over a ten-year period. For projects in which no federal financing is provided, the tax credit is 9% per year for ten years. If a qualifying project uses federal financing, the tax credit is 4% per year for ten years.

The tax credit is available for units rented to low-income occupants. To qualify, (a) at least 20% of a project's units must be rented to households with incomes of 50% or less of the area median income, or (b) at least 40% of the units must be rented to households with incomes of 60% or less of the area median income.

Owners must keep the rental units available to low-income tenants for at least thirty years to qualify for the LIHTC. In allocating LIHTCs, the IRS requires that projects that serve the lowest-income tenants and guarantee low rent for the longest period of time are given priority. A common technique used to obtain a competitive advantage in bidding for LIHTCs is to agree that the rental units will remain available to low-income tenants for thirty-one or more years.

While developers may certainly use the LIHTCs to reduce their federal income tax liability, a valuable feature of the LIHTC is that it is assignable. It can be purchased by investors with no direct involvement in the development process. This feature gives the LIHTC market value that can be used to raise capital to construct affordable housing projects for low-income occupants.

In a common scenario, LIHTCs from several projects will be pooled and sold through a syndication process, with the investors receiving the benefits of the LIHTCs and often receiving a limited partnership interest in the housing project. By being able to sell LIHTCs, a developer that has received an allocation of LIHTCs for an eligible low-income housing project can raise up-front capital to construct new buildings or rehabilitate existing buildings into affordable housing.

Among projects that qualify for LIHTCs are brownfield projects involving the conversion of former warehouse and factory brownfield sites into affordable housing. As an added bonus, it is permissible to combine LIHTCs with Federal Historic Preservation Tax Incentives when a low-income housing project is to be located in a building with certified historic significance or a qualifying building built before 1936.

With this in mind, consider the economic advantage to a developer redeveloping a historic building as low-income housing. The developer can receive a 20% historic preservation tax credit in the year the project is placed in service plus receive an additional 9% tax credit that year (for an aggregate 29% tax credit the year the project is placed in service) as well as a 9% tax credit for each of the following nine (9) years. That represents potential tax credits over ten (10) years with a face value aggregating 110% of the cost of the project. Even applying a present value discount, that represents very close to the developer's entire project development costs being recovered through tax credits alone.

The same calculus applies to redevelopment of nonhistoric buildings built before 1936 as low-income housing, except that the first year tax credit aggregates 19% instead of 29%.

This is an extraordinarily powerful incentive to recycle historic and nonhistoric buildings built before 1936 as low-income housing. It's a wonder that more developers are not taking advantage of this opportunity.

For more information on use of LIHTCs for urban redevelopment, contact

> National Low Income Housing Coalition
> 727 15th St. NW, 6th Floor
> Washington DC 20005
> 202-662-1530
> *www.nlihc.org*

According to the U.S. Department of Housing and Urban Development (HUD), "[t]he Low Income Housing Tax Credit (LIHTC) is the most important resource for creating affordable housing in the United States today."

For more information on the LIHTC Program, contact HUD at

HUD User
PO Box 23268
Washington DC 20026-3268
800-245-2691
TDD 800-927-7589
Fax 202-708-9981
*helpdesk@huduser.org*

The LIHTC allocating agencies in Illinois are the Illinois Housing Development Authority (IHDA) and the city of Chicago. IHDA allocates LIHTCs on a competitive basis throughout the state, including the city of Chicago. The city of Chicago, through its Department of Housing, allocates LIHTCs on a competitive basis for projects only within the city of Chicago.

The Illinois Housing Development Authority contact for information concerning low-income housing tax credits is

Shelly Tucciarilli
Manager of Tax Credits for Multifamily Housing
Multifamily Finance Department
Illinois Housing Development Authority
401 North Michigan Avenue, Suite 700
Chicago IL 60611
312-836-5333
TDD: 312-836-5222
*stucciar@ihda.org*
*www.ihda.org*

# New Markets Tax Credits—Federal

The New Markets Tax Credit (NMTC) Program was created through the Community Renewal Tax Relief Act of 2000, codified at IRS Code Section 45(D), and is administered by the Community Development Financial Institutions (CDFI) Fund under the U.S. Department of Treasury. The purpose of the NMTC Program is to expand availability of credit, investment capital, and financial services in economically distressed communities. Current funding authorization is to allocate $3.5 billion dollars per year. New market tax credits are allocated by the CDFI to various approved Community Development Entities (CDE). Under the NMTC program, a CDE is defined as "any duly organized entity treated as a domestic corporation or partnership for federal income tax purposes that: (a) has a primary mission of serving, or providing investment capital for, low-income communities or low-income persons; (b) maintains accountability to residents of low-income communities through their representation on any governing board of the entity or any advisory board to the entity; and (c) has been certified as a CDE by the CDFI Fund of the US Department of Treasury."

Once a CDE has been allocated NMTCs, the credits can be offered to investors in exchange for financing redevelopment projects and for stock or other equity interest in a CDE project. The NMTC amounts to a tax credit totaling 39% of the investor's investment cost, to be claimed over a seven-year credit allowance period—5% per year for the first three years and 6% per year for the last four years. An investor is locked into the investment for a minimum of seven years and cannot redeem its investment until after the seven-year period expires.

To qualify to receive NMTCs, a CDE must be certified by the CDFI Fund. Once certified, a CDE may make various types of investments in low-income communities, including loans or investments in real estate projects involving brownfield cleanup and redevelopment.

Creation of a CDE to obtain NMTCs is a viable approach for raising capital to fund brownfield projects in low-income communities where many brownfields are located. Both for-profit and not-for-profit entities may qualify for CDE certification. Once certified as a CDE, the designation lasts for the life of the organization.

For more information about NMTCs or to obtain information and application materials to become certified as a CDE, contact

> United States Department of the Treasury
> Community Development Financial Institutions Fund
> 601 Thirteenth St., NW, Suite 200 South
> Washington DC 20005
> *www.cdfifund.gov*

> CDFI Help Desk
> 202-622-6355
> *cdfihelp@cdfi.treas.gov*

> New Market Tax Credits support line
> 202-622-6355

*The IRS Circular 230 Disclosure included in chapter 21 applies throughout this chapter.*

## Other Incentives and Economic Resources

For other areas of interest potentially beneficial to brownfield site redevelopment, consider the following sources:

a. Internal Revenue Service Publication 954, *Tax Incentives for Empowerment Zones and Other Distressed Communities,* available at *www.irs.gov/formspubs/index.html.*

163

b. Income and estate tax deductions for charitable contributions of interests in historic property under the Tax Reform Act of 1986— potentially useful as an incentive to induce taxpayers to consider charitable donation of brownfield sites with historic significance to a qualified charitable organization to obtain a tax deduction.

c. U.S. Department of Housing and Urban Development—can provide funds or loan guarantees for certain qualified brownfield projects providing affordable housing to low- to moderate-income occupants under its Community Development Block Grant Program and Section 108 Loan Program. See *www.hud.gov/offices/cpd/communitydevelopment/programs/108/#maximum.*

d. HUD Brownfield Economic Development Initiative—provides grants to help cities redevelop abandoned and underused commercial and industrial brownfields, *www.hud.gov/offices/cpd/economicdevelopment/programs/bedi/index.cfm.*

e. HUD Community Development Block Grants—provides annual funding for activities by cities, counties, and states to promote economic redevelopment and revitalization of distressed communities, often including a number of brownfields, *www.hud.gov/offices/cpd/communitydevelopment/programs/index.cfm.*

f. U.S. Department of Transportation, Community, and System Preservation Program—provides funds to states, local governments, planning organizations, and tribal governments to integrate transportation plans with community development objectives, useful for large-scale projects in communities with transportation infrastructure issues, *www.fhwa.dot.gov/tcsp.*

A vast array of other government assistance programs exists designed to provide economic assistance to specific types of redevelopment projects, such as public works, economic development facilities, water/sewer/storm drainage and solid waste facilities, rural development, urban and community forestry programs, targeted brownfield assessments, etc. New programs are created yearly, and new and creative ways to expand existing programs to fund brownfield cleanup and redevelopment are constantly evolving.

If brownfield contamination will impact the cost of a redevelopment project, a diligent inquiry into available public funding for brownfield assessment and cleanup based on the specifics of the project is appropriate.

If the costs associated with brownfield assessment and cleanup are standing in the way of an otherwise economically desirable brownfield redevelopment project, ascertaining the availability of public funds to reduce or eliminate those costs makes a huge amount of sense.

Once a project development concept plan is in place, part of the due diligence analysis of the project should include an evaluation of available public funds to pay for or reduce financing costs that would otherwise be payable by the developer. The analysis of available programs should not be limited to those set forth in this chapter. Available funding for brownfield redevelopment is ever changing. Funds allocated for a program today may be cut tomorrow. New programs may be developed. Funding for old programs may be replenished or expanded.

If the proposed brownfield development project accomplishes a legitimate public objective, public funds may be available to enhance profitability to a private developer. The *public* objective can be as general as needed economic development. If the case can be made that the needed economic development will not occur in the absence of public economic incentives granted to a private developer, the stage is set to obtain public money for private development.

# 23

# Section 1031 Exchange Basics

What if I told you that you could get a hefty 0% interest loan from the federal government to invest in commercial or industrial real estate? Would you be interested? Better yet, what if that loan has no fixed monthly, quarterly, or annual repayment obligations and does not show up on your credit report or balance sheet as an outstanding liability? Still better yet, what if the terms of the loan provide that it may never have to be repaid? Are you interested now?

In effect,[1] that's what a Section 1031 exchange can do for you. Here's how:

Section 1031 of the Internal Revenue Code permits a taxpayer to dispose of property used in its trade or business or held for investment purposes without paying federal income taxes, including capital gains taxes, on any gain arising from the transaction. To qualify for nonrecognition of gain, the taxpayer disposing of the qualifying property must comply with the technical requirements of Section 1031 by exchanging the property for other *like-kind* property within the time period provided by the statute. In

---

[1] Apologies to my conservative friends who will point out that tax relief is not a loan from the government, but rather a nontaking of your money.

general, that time period is 180 days but may be cut short if the taxpayer files its tax return for the period in which the Section 1031 exchange was initiated before the 180-day period expires. The key Section 1031 exchange rules are outlined later in this chapter.

To demonstrate the value of a Section 1031 exchange, I want to focus on the concept that a Section 1031 exchange permits you to dispose of qualifying property without being obligated to pay federal income taxes on any gain arising from the transaction. It works like this:

*Scenario number 1.* Suppose you bought a parcel of vacant ground for $100,000, with the intent to use the parcel in your trade or business or simply to hold for investment purposes. A few years later, you decide to sell the parcel, which has risen in value to $300,000. Upon sale, you will have a taxable gain of $200,000.

Assume a federal capital gains tax rate of 15%. (There may also be applicable state taxes that can be deferred.) This is an appropriate assumption at the time this book is written, although President Barack Obama has indicated he may seek to increase the capital gains tax rate to 25%. Such an increase will make use of a Section 1031 exchange even more valuable. Even if no changes are made to the current tax code, the capital gains rate is scheduled to increase to 20% on January 1, 2011.

At a 15% capital gains rate, the federal income tax payable in scenario number 1 is $30,000 (15% x $200,000 = $30,000). If you held the property free and clear with no mortgage, you would be left with $270,000, which could be used to acquire another property ($300,000 sale price-$30,000 capital gains tax = $270,000). As the tax rate on capital gains increases, the amount remaining after taxes for reinvestment decreases. For instance, if the capital gains tax rate is increased to 25%, the tax on the $200,000 gain would increase to $50,000, leaving you only $250,000 available to reinvest.

*Scenario number 2.* Suppose instead of purchasing a parcel of vacant property, as assumed in scenario number 1, you bought a parcel of improved real estate. Suppose the purchase price was $500,000, with $100,000 allocated to the land and $400,000 allocated to building improvements. Ten years later, you sell the property for $700,000. During the ten-year period you owned the property, you deducted $100,000 as depreciation expense.

Although the property is sold for $200,000 more than your purchase price, the gain you realize is actually $300,000 because the $100,000 accumulated depreciation deduction reduces the property's tax basis by a corresponding amount. As a consequence, although you purchased the property for $500,000, the current tax basis (after depreciation) is only $400,000. Therefore, the taxable gain is $300,000, calculated by deducting the tax basis from the sale price.

At first glance, you may believe that the effect of the foregoing is to increase your capital gain to $300,000 resulting in a tax of $45,000 (15% x $300,000 = $45,000); but that is not correct. Under current tax law, you are required to first pay a tax on an amount equal to the accumulated depreciation taken as a deduction on the property, at a depreciation recapture tax rate of $25%, with the balance of the gain taxed at the assumed 15% capital gains rate. As a consequence, the tax you will owe is $55,000 (25% x $100,000 depreciation recapture = $25,000, plus 15% x $200,000 capital gain = $30,000, for a total tax of $55,000). If we once again assume for simplicity that you did not have a mortgage on the property, you would be left with $645,000 to reinvest in another property.

The beauty of a Section 1031 exchange of like-kind property is that the gain on the transactions described in scenario number 1 and scenario number 2 is not recognized at the time of sale, with the result that you do not have to pay either capital gains tax or depreciation recapture taxes on the transaction. Consequently, in scenario number 1, you will have the whole $300,000 to reinvest; and in scenario number 2, you will have the whole $700,000 to reinvest.

The capital gains taxes and the depreciation recapture taxes are not *waived* by use of a Section 1031 exchange, but rather, the obligation to pay these taxes is deferred until a future transaction that results in a taxable event that recognizes a gain. Since there is no prohibition against utilizing the Section 1031 exchange procedure in successive transactions, payment of taxes on the gain can be deferred indefinitely. If the taxpayer is a limited liability company, corporation, trust, or other entity with a perpetual existence, the day of reckoning for payment of the capital gains taxes and depreciation recapture taxes may never come. You will, however, limit your depreciation deduction because the tax basis of the relinquished property will carry over as the tax basis of the replacement property. This tax basis can be adjusted upward if additional capital is contributed to acquire the replacement property or, thereafter, to improve the replacement property.

If the taxpayer/exchangor is a natural person rather than a limited liability company, corporation, trust, or other independent legal entity, the Internal Revenue Code provides that upon the death of the taxpayer/exchangor, the tax basis of all property owned by the taxpayer is *stepped up* to the property's fair market value as of the date of death. As a consequence, no capital gains tax or depreciation recapture taxes will ever be recognized on the prior exchanges.

It is these attributes that form the basis of my statement at the outset of this chapter that it is possible to, in effect, obtain a long-term loan from the federal government, without interest, without scheduled periodic payments, without reflecting an outstanding liability on your credit report or balance sheet, and, possibly, with no obligation to ever repay. It is not a perfect analogy, but you get the point.

There are a whole host of technical rules that apply to Section 1031 exchanges. For this reason, advice from a knowledgeable tax advisor is critical when structuring a Section 1031 exchange.

As the title of this chapter suggests, it is intended to give you only the basics. The purpose of this chapter is to alert you to the potential value and benefit of structuring your *sale* transaction as a Section 1031 exchange.

The following is an outline of key rules applicable to Section 1031 exchanges. Become familiar with these rules. Unless you intend to completely cash out of real estate investing, a Section 1031 exchange may work to your benefit. If you intend to keep investing in real estate or using real estate in your trade or business, a Section 1031 exchange will maximize the capital you have available to reinvest.

## *Key Elements of a Section 1031 Exchange*

What is Section 1031?

Section 1031 refers to Section 1031 of the Internal Revenue Code.

What does it do?

Section 1031 permits a taxpayer (the *Exchangor*) to dispose of certain real estate and personal property and replace it with *like-kind* property without being required to pay taxes on the transaction.

What property qualifies?

To qualify for a Section 1031 exchange, the property being disposed of (the *Relinquished Property*) must have been used in the Exchangor's trade or business and/or must have been held for investment purposes. The property being acquired (the *Replacement Property*) must likewise be acquired for use in the Exchangor's trade or business or for investment.

**What property is considered *like-kind*?**

To be *like-kind* means simply that real estate must be exchanged for real estate, and personal property must be exchanged for personal property. Personal property is any property that is not real estate.

For example, a warehouse may be exchanged for another warehouse or for any other qualifying real estate including, for instance, a factory building, office building, shopping center, single-tenant store, parking garage, or even a parcel of vacant ground so long as it qualifies as being acquired for use in the Exchangor's trade or business or is to be held for investment. This is not a difficult test to pass. Similarly, a qualifying parcel of vacant ground or a shopping center or office building or factory or other parcels of investment real estate may be exchanged for any other qualifying real estate investment.

Similarly, subject to certain exclusions, qualifying equipment and other personal property used in a trade or business or held for investment purposes may be exchanged for other qualifying equipment or personal property for use in a trade or business or to be held for investment purposes.

What property is excluded? The following types of property do not qualify for a Section 1031 exchange: stocks, bonds, partnership interests, limited liability company interests, personal residences, and stocks in trade or inventory.

Are there timing issues? Section 1031 exchanges can be simultaneous, but they are not required to be. In fact, most exchanges made pursuant to Section 1031 are not simultaneous. There are, however, strict timing rules that apply to nonsimultaneous exchanges and strict rules prohibiting access to funds.

What are the time limits? The Replacement Property or properties must be identified, in writing, not later than forty-five days after the Relinquished Property is transferred (the *Identification Period*). The Replacement Property or properties must be acquired not later than the earlier of (i) 180 days after the Relinquished Property was transferred, or (ii) the due date for the Exchangor's tax return, including any extensions (the *Acquisition Period*). The Identification Period is included within the Acquisition Period.

How many Replacement
Properties may be identified? There is no fixed limit to the number of Replacement Properties that may be identified, but there are three rules that apply:

(1) the Three-Property Rule, (2) the 200% Rule, and (3) the 95% Rule.

1.  The Three-Property Rule allows you to identify up to three (3) properties as potential Replacement Properties, regardless of value. You need not acquire all three properties, but as of the end of the Identification Period, not more than three properties may be identified. This is the most commonly used identification rule.

2.  The 200% Rule allows you to identify any number of potential Replacement Properties so long as the aggregate value of all identified properties does not exceed 200% of the value of the Relinquished Property. You need not acquire all identified properties.

3.  The 95% Rule allows you to identify any number of potential Replacement Properties, regardless of value so long as you actually acquire within the Acquisition Period at least 95% of the value of all properties identified.

Must all exchange proceeds be used?

There is no requirement that all proceeds received upon sale of the Relinquished Property be used to acquire the Replacement

Property. Any exchange proceeds not used, however, are taxable.

What constitutes exchange proceeds?

Exchange proceeds means the net sale price of the Relinquished Property, including all net equity and the amount of any mortgage encumbering the Relinquished Property, whether paid off at closing or assumed by the purchaser. It is not sufficient to merely reinvest the net equity received upon sale. The purchase price of the Replacement Property must equal or exceed the aggregate of the net equity received upon sale of the Relinquished Property plus any mortgage encumbering the Relinquished Property at the time of the sale closing.

*Example:* If the Relinquished Property is encumbered by a $700,000 mortgage and is sold for $1 million as part of a Section 1031 exchange transaction, to defer all taxes, the purchase price of the Replacement Property must be at least $1 million, not merely $300,000.

When can the Exchang or obtain access to unused proceeds?

Proceeds from sale of the Relinquished Property may be accessed only when the exchange is completed, fails, or expires. If no potential Replacement Properties are identified within the Identification Period, the exchange fails, and the Exchangor may receive the funds. Those funds will, however, be taxed in the year received. If all properties identified within the Identification Period are acquired within the Acquisition Period, the exchange is completed, and any remaining funds may be received by the Exchangor. Those remaining funds are taxable. If less than all identified properties are acquired, but the Acquisition Period expires, all remaining funds may be received by the Exchangor, but are taxable.

These are the basics. As tax rates rise, Section 1031 exchanges will become increasingly valuable.

A Section 1031 exchange is not a new and exotic tax shelter scheme. Tax deferred exchanges of like-kind property have been recognized by the Internal Revenue Service as a valid tax deferral strategy since the early 1920s. The structure and effect of a Section 1031 exchange were specifically authorized by Congress by enacting Section 1031 of the Internal Revenue Code, and the Internal Revenue Service has promulgated extensive regulations for its implementation.

*The IRS Circular 230 Disclosure included in chapter 21 applies to this chapter.*

Use Section 1031 to your advantage, and prosper.

## 24

# Money from Thin Air: Developing Urban Air Rights

Prime commercial land is limited. Prices per square foot can be astronomical. Demand for efficiency to maximize return is growing. No wonder developers and property owners are looking to the sky, with varying degrees of success, to capture all the value they can from each urban parcel.

Owners and developers, and people in general, are conditioned to think of potential development sites as flat surfaces with essentially two dimensions: north/south and east/west. They see only the surface of the land and envision the building they will construct for the particular purpose they have in mind: a bank, a drugstore, a restaurant, a strip mall, a parking garage, an office building. If the parcel is larger than they need, they may envision subdividing the parcel to make two or more lots. In most cases, however, they think primarily in terms of land coverage for the type of building they need. They visualize only the two-dimensional space depicted on their site plan or plat of survey.

In thirty out of fifty states, including all Midwestern states, the Public Land Survey System (PLSS) is in effect. The PLSS has its roots in the Land Ordinance of 1785 and the Northwest Ordinance of 1787, establishing a rectangular survey system to meet the needs of the federal government as it faced the challenge of dividing vast areas of undeveloped land lying west of the original thirteen colonies. The system, developed under the direction of Thomas Jefferson, essentially divides the United States into rectangles, measured in relation to lines known as meridians and base lines.

Development lots are instinctively viewed as the two-dimensional surface of land visually representing a potential development parcel. Descriptions of a parcel typically refer to "a parcel of land X feet by Y feet" located in relation to an intersection or other identifiable landmark.

Once a parcel is *developed*, or designated for development, by construction of improvements on the land, it is natural to think of the parcel as being unavailable for further development (unless the existing improvements are to be demolished).

Classic examples of this are single-story commercial buildings at prime commercial locations, a multideck parking garage or mid-rise building in a downtown development area, railroad tracks or spurs cutting across valuable urban land, and, in some cases, roadways and alleys.

Each of these situations represent, potentially, underutilization of valuable real estate. Finding a way to develop the *air* above these existing or planned improvements maximizes the economic utility of these parcels and can be like creating *money from thin air*.

The practice of finding ways to utilize the *space above* is often referred to as *air rights development*. Air rights development requires thinking in three dimensions and requires serious design consideration and legal planning, but when land values are at a premium and zoning permits, the economic return may be dramatic.

Though often overlooked, virtually all of Chicago's downtown business district is a "city in the air." People tend to think of streets and street-level entrances to buildings in the downtown Chicago Loop as being at *ground level*. This is simply not the case. Most of what is thought of in the Chicago Loop as being at *ground level* is located twelve to twenty-two feet above the earth's surface. This explains the vast network of *lower* streets and passageways in downtown Chicago, such as *Lower Wacker Drive*, *Lower Dearborn Street*, Lower State Street, etc., which most people seldom traverse. It also explains why, in 1992, the Chicago Loop business district was virtually shut down by "the Great Loop Flood of '92," but few people got wet or even saw any water as office and retail buildings were closed and workers were sent home because of *flooding*.

The point of these observations is to reveal that development of air rights is not new. It is also not "some exotic legal manipulation of doubtful efficacy dreamed up by big city lawyers for use only in big cities." Development of so-called *air rights* is little more than efficient use of a limited resource when use becomes economically feasible and beneficial.

*Air rights* are part of the *bundle of rights* constituting fee simple title to real estate. The term *air rights* generally refers to the right of the owner of fee simple title of a parcel of land to use the space above the land. If this right did not exist, it would not be possible to construct improvements on the land, such as a home, fence, or other structure above the surface of the land. While the ancient common law doctrine that "ownership of land extends to the periphery of the universe" has been limited to accommodate the modern-world realities of air travel, the fundamental concept that land ownership includes the right to use and occupy the airspace above the surface of the land is well established. See *United States v. Causby, 326 US, 256, 261-266 (1946).*

As one of the bundle of property rights comprising fee simple title to real estate, *air rights* may also be *unbundled* and alienated separate from other rights in the bundle. Conceptually, from a legal standpoint, the separation and transfer of so-called *air rights* is not materially different from subdividing and transferring a lot pictured in only two dimensions. Instead of subdividing and selling off, for example, "that part of Lot 1 lying east of the west 100 feet of Lot 1" as depicted on a plat of survey, the transfer of air rights subdivides and transfers a parcel based upon its vertical elevation. For example, one might subdivide and transfer "that part of Lot 1 lying above a horizontal plane located 100 feet above [some benchmark elevation]."

In Chicago, Illinois, the benchmark is Chicago City Datum, which, for vertical elevations, represents *zero feet*. The Chicago Municipal Code (10-4-210) defines Chicago's City Datum as "a plane 17.640 feet below the benchmark cut on top of the bottom stone of granite base at the southeast corner of the Northern Trust Company Bank Building at the northwest corner of S. LaSalle Street and W. Monroe Street." A brass plaque facing Monroe Street on the cornerstone of the Northern Trust Company Bank Building at this location memorializes the Chicago City Datum benchmark.

By dividing a development parcel *vertically*, it is often possible to stack uses in a mixed-use development owned by more than one owner or developer, in the same way it is possible to subdivide and develop side by side a horizontal surface subdivision. In some cases, without even developing the open air above existing or planned improvements, it is possible to sell and transfer *air rights* to an adjacent property owner to allow construction of a taller building on an adjacent building site. Recognizing this potential can result in a substantial economic windfall to a property owner otherwise underutilizing a valuable development parcel.

Air rights development is a combination of black letter real estate law and the applicable zoning code of the community in which your property is located. Because zoning codes are legislative pronouncements, they are subject to change as local city councils determine appropriate. For this reason, the current zoning classification for every project, and certainly for any project involving *air rights development*, must be examined at the beginning of each transaction as part of the due diligence investigation.

Case in point: The Chicago Zoning Ordinance was amended effective August 1, 2004, not long after I published the original article upon which this chapter is based. The zoning code amendments changed the zoning classifications of many properties, especially affecting downtown Chicago. I considered rewriting the hypotheticals used in this chapter to reflect the new zoning classifications but decided to add this caveat instead. Whenever dealing with any urban property, it is critical to check current zoning and its characteristics as part of your project due diligence in every case. They are legislative pronouncements and are subject to change—sometimes drastically. This chapter is not intended as a determinative analysis of the Chicago Zoning Ordinance. The point of this chapter is to explore *air rights development* in general. The Chicago Zoning Ordinance changed on August 1, 2004, and it may change again whenever the city council and mayor determine a change is appropriate. The zoning code in your own city or town will have its own classifications and characteristics. The principals of air rights development remain the same even as the particulars of each classification change. Check your applicable zoning ordinance before you proceed.

Hypothetical Facts: Suppose you are planning to acquire a twenty-thousand-square-foot parcel in Chicago, Illinois, zoned (preamendment) B6-6. Your purchase price is $4.5 million. You believe it is a perfect location for a restaurant/entertainment complex serving food and liquor, with live entertainment and dancing. You visualize a state-of-the-art venue spread out over two floors, with about nineteen thousand square feet of usable space per floor, for a total restaurant/entertainment venue of thirty-eight thousand square feet. Fortunately, adequate parking is close by and available. Demand for offices and condominium housing is growing in the vicinity of your parcel, which you believe will further enhance the chances of success of your planned business by bringing more customers through your doors. Although you recognize development of offices and condominiums in your area is a *hot* development opportunity and might also be an excellent investment, you have no interest or experience in developing offices or condominiums and really just want to develop and open your dream restaurant/entertainment complex. You have calculated your costs of construction and operation and believe the project is economically feasible, although you would like to find a way to cut your costs or otherwise increase your return on investment.

Consider this: The restaurant/entertainment complex you wish to construct is a permitted use in the (preamendment) B6-6 zoning classification under the Chicago Zoning Ordinance. Also permitted is a wide array of other business and service uses, as well as dwelling units as long as the dwelling units are not below the second floor.

The permitted floor area ratio (FAR) for a parcel zoned (pre-amendment) B6-6 under the Chicago Zoning Ordinance is 12, which means that the total square footage of the building or buildings permitted on your 20,000-square-foot parcel is 240,000 square feet. You are utilizing only 38,000 square feet, which means, from a zoning standpoint at least, you are underutilizing your parcel to the extent of 202,000 square feet.

Suppose you were able to reconfigure your proposed project to free up 1,000 to 1,200 square feet per floor in return for recovering half (or more) of your total land cost. If this were possible, your restaurant/entertainment complex may be reduced in size to 36,000 square feet instead of 38,000 square feet, but your development cost for the project might be reduced $2.5 million or more. Almost free money.

How could this work?

*Scenario number 1.* With the hypothetical facts presented, it is certainly within the realm of possibilities to market and sell the *airspace* above your proposed restaurant/entertainment complex for development of offices and/or condominiums. As mentioned, under the applicable zoning classification, 202,000 square feet remains available for development on your site. With prevailing land values of $225 per square foot (represented by your purchase price of $4.5 million for a 20,000-square-foot parcel), a condominium/office developer may well view your airspace parcel as a bargain at $2.5 million ($125 per square foot—measured in two dimensions for 20,000 square feet) since it would still enable construction of 202,000 square feet of floor area above the second floor.

Obviously, to make the *airspace* usable, adequate means of access and support must be planned, which will require detailed planning for design and construction of both the ground-level parcel and the *airspace* parcel (which do not necessarily need to be constructed at the same time, although simultaneous construction may be more efficient and practical) and creation of legally sufficient easements of support and easements for ingress and egress, utilities, loading and unloading, mail delivery, a street-level lobby, elevators, standpipes, etc., as well as drafting of development-specific covenants running with the land to promote noninterference and compatibility of use of each parcel. The necessity for easements of support, and easements (or conveyance of fee parcels) for a street-level lobby, mail-delivery areas, and loading and unloading areas, is the reason slight reduction in size of the proposed restaurant/entertainment complex is suggested in the premise to scenario number 1—to free up space for these purposes.

While sale of an *air rights parcel* will require added expense for engineering (much of which will likely be undertaken by the proposed developer of the air rights parcel) and attorney's fees to negotiate and draft a workable declaration of easements, covenants, and restrictions to legally facilitate the development and use of each parcel, the economic advantage of being able to sell the air rights parcel may more than justify the added effort and development expense involved.

*Scenario number 2.* Assume the same hypothetical facts as in scenario number 1, except that instead of being the owner of the parcel referred to in scenario number 1 (the *entertainment parcel*), you own or wish to develop a parcel adjacent to the entertainment parcel. Perhaps the entertainment parcel has already been developed with the restaurant/entertainment complex referred to in scenario number 1. Assume your parcel (the *high-rise parcel*) is 40,000 square feet with (preamendment) B6-6 zoning, and you wish to construct (or to sell your parcel to a developer to construct) a mixed-use development with first-floor retail, five floors of office space, and six floors of luxury condominiums. Because zoning for the high-rise parcel allows a FAR of 12, you determine a twelve-story, 480,000-square-foot building is the maximum you will be able to construct on your 40,000-square-foot lot.

In conducting a financial analysis of your project, you determine that the marginal cost of each floor would result in you generating a substantially greater return on your investment if you were able to construct additional floors of office space, condominiums, or even multilevel parking in your proposed project on the high-rise parcel. Still, you are faced with the maximum FAR of 12 for the high-rise parcel as established by the Chicago Zoning Ordinance.

Is there a solution? Perhaps.

The Chicago Zoning Ordinance defines a *zoning lot* as follows: "A 'zoning lot or lots' is a single tract of land located within a single block, which (at the time of filing for a building permit) is designated by its owner or developer as a tract to be used, developed, or built upon as a unit, under single ownership or control. Therefore, 'zoning lot or lots' may or may not coincide with a lot of record."

One solution is that the owner of the high-rise parcel might acquire the *air rights* over the entertainment parcel (by purchasing from the owner of the entertainment parcel "all of the entertainment parcel except that part thereof lying below a horizontal plane located x feet above the Chicago City Datum") and then designate the entertainment parcel as part of the zoning lot to be developed and controlled by the developer of the high-rise parcel. The *zoning lot* would then be 60,000 square feet. Because the FAR remains 12, the maximum floor area on the total zoning lot is 720,000 square feet.

Because 38,000 square feet has been used (or is to be used) for the restaurant/entertainment complex, 682,000 square feet remains available for development on the zoning lot (being, in effect, the high-rise parcel). Therefore, instead of being able to construct only a 480,000-square-foot project on the high-rise parcel, if developed alone, the developer would now be able to construct up to an additional 202,000 square feet (for a total of 682,000 square feet) on the high-rise parcel—or, roughly, five additional floors at 40,000 square feet each because the high-rise parcel and the entertainment parcel, collectively, constitute the *zoning lot*. Note that FAR does not dictate building height; it dictates floor area. Particularly, it establishes the ratio of building floor area to the size of the zoning lot. There is no requirement that a building built on a zoning lot must cover the entire lot. Accordingly, assuming there is no separate municipal height restriction or other applicable bulk restriction that limits building height (which sometimes there is, so you must check this out with your city or town) on zoning parcel with a FAR of 12, you could build a twelve-story story building covering the entire lot or an eighteen-story building covering two-thirds of the lot or a twenty-four-story building covering one-half the lot, etc. FAR is simply the ratio of building square feet to total square footage of the entire zoning lot—nothing more, nothing less.

*   *   *

Of course, if the developer does construct 682,000 square feet of floor area on the high-rise parcel (in addition to the 38,000 square feet constructed on the entertainment parcel) under the foregoing scenario number 2, all floor area available for development of the combined zoning lot pursuant to the zoning ordinance will have been fully utilized. As a result, since the zoning lot is fully developed as a whole, no further opportunity exists to expand the square footage of improvements on the entertainment parcel. If the restaurant/entertainment complex fails or is destroyed or otherwise demolished, the replacement improvements will be limited to a maximum square footage of 38,000 square feet.

To avoid this outcome, parties will sometimes negotiate an *air rights transfer* that raises the elevation of the delimiting horizontal plane and includes an express covenant running with the land that reserves potential floor area to the transferring parcel (in this case, the entertainment parcel).

To do this, the instrument of transfer may provide, for example, that the delimiting horizontal plane is 20 to 30 feet higher than previously indicated and may include an appurtenant covenant specifying that the owner of the high-rise parcel may not construct more than 640,000 square feet of floor area on the high-rise parcel. This would result in added development potential for the high-rise parcel being reduced by approximately one floor of 40,000 square feet (since only 640,000 square feet of floor area would be allowed instead of 682,000), but would also reserve to the entertainment parcel the opportunity to construct a total of 80,000 square feet of floor area—or roughly four stories—for a building approximately twice the size of the currently planned restaurant/entertainment complex.

Reserving square footage for future development of the entertainment parcel may impact the value of the *air rights* being sold (if the owner of the high-rise parcel intends to use the full extent of available FAR), but it also provides flexibility for future development of the entertainment parcel.

Under scenario number 2, the sale of *air rights* is more akin to the sale of *development rights*, but the legal principal is substantially the same as in scenario number 1. In each case, a property owner is selling the right to develop *the sky above* while retaining the ground-level development parcel.

*   *   *

*Air rights* are valuable property rights that can be sold, purchased, mortgaged, and transferred. Under the right circumstances, *air rights* may represent a substantial untapped resource with great value to those who recognize their potential. Since the transfer of these property rights may not directly impair the owner's intended use of the surface level property, they often do represent *money from thin air*.

# 25

# When *Wraparound Mortgages* Return: The Time to Plan Is *Now*

With interest rates near historic lows, commercial real estate is, for the second time this decade, being financed at rates few believed possible before September 11, 2001. Credit standards have tightened following the crash of the residential subprime lending market in March 2007. The commercial real estate industry avoided the impact of subprime lending fallout for much of 2007, but commercial lending has tightened in 2008 as credit markets have paused to see where our economy is headed. Many commercial credit underwriters are sitting on the sidelines, waiting for a sign that the worst of the credit market fiasco is over. Still, there are lenders with money to lend who are scrambling to find borrowers and are willing to be flexible to attract borrowers with fiscally sound commercial real estate projects. Capital does not earn a profit unless it is put to work.

## Planning for Rising Rates

Forward-thinking investors and developers with fiscally sound projects will use this time wisely to negotiate loan terms, enabling them to take advantage of today's low interest rates when interest rates rise.

*Now* is the time to plan for the future. *Now* is the time for investors to lock in attractive loan rates for extended periods, if possible, and to make sure they have the flexibility to keep those rates when economic conditions and future needs change.

*Investors:* Now is the time to negotiate provisions in your commercial real estate mortgage to allow you to leverage current low interest rates to your advantage when interest rates rise. Here's how:

## Leveraging Low Interest Rates

In one respect, the value of locking in low interest rates for extended periods when interest rates are likely to rise is obvious. If you knew today that interest rates were rising and that in the foreseeable future interest rates were going to be 7.5%, 8.5%, 9.5%, or higher, who wouldn't lock in today's low interest rates if they could? That is not really the issue. That concept is self-evident.

But what if, for example, you lock in a low interest rate today for the next ten, twenty, or thirty years, interest rates rise significantly, and then, say five or six years from now, you wish to sell your investment?

Assuming prepayment of your loan is allowed, one solution is to simply sell the property. In this case, you would receive your equity and would be free to reinvest at then-prevailing returns. Unless you have a *portable mortgage* allowing substitution of collateral and transfer to a new project, you would promptly lose any future benefit of your long-term low interest rate because the project would be gone and, most likely, the mortgage paid off.

If the mortgage is *assumable*, you may gain some advantage by being able to negotiate a higher sale price for the project because the assuming buyer will be able to benefit from your lower rate. An obvious problem with this scenario is that if the project has appreciated substantially, the amount of the down payment the buyer may be required to produce to pay the equity between the purchase price and the remaining loan balance may be prohibitive to most buyers, thereby reducing demand for your property and creating downward pressure to lower the price.

Are there other solutions?

Consider the following hypothetical facts:

Today: Investor acquires an office building, strip shopping center, single-use building, or other typical investment property (the *property*) for $2 million. Investor obtains a loan for $1.5 million (75% loan to value) with a fixed interest rate of 6.25 % amortized and payable over twenty years, secured by a first mortgage on the property.

Five years later: Now, project yourself five years into the future. Interest rates on first mortgage loans have risen to 9.5%. Interest rates on loans secured by second position mortgages are, perhaps, 10.5% to 11%. Because of built-in rental increases under existing leases, the property has appreciated in value to, say, $2.2 million. Perhaps the tax shelter benefits of the property to the investor have diminished somewhat because the investor used segregated cost accounting to accelerate cost recovery in the early years of the investment, so the investor has decided to sell. The sale price is $2.2 million.

*Case number 1.* Investor could simply sell the property to a willing buyer (the *buyer*) who would be responsible for obtaining its own financing. Under a typical scenario, the buyer will obtain a mortgage loan for 75% of the value of the property at current market interest rates. Under the hypothetical facts given, the buyer will invest equity of $550,000.00 (25% of the purchase price) and will obtain a first mortgage loan in the amount of $1.65 million (75% of value) at a current interest rate of 9.5% amortized over twenty years, with a fifteen-year balloon payment. The buyer's monthly payment would be $15,380.16. The balloon payment due in fifteen years would be $732,323.88. The original investor would cash out at the time of funding this loan, and the original first mortgage loan would be paid off.

*Case number 2.* If the mortgage is *assumable* (or, at least, not due-on-sale), the buyer could, if it chose to do so and the seller agrees, pay the original investor an amount equal to the investor's equity in the property and *assume* or *take subject to* the mortgage obligation with its low 6.25% interest rate for the balance of fifteen years. If this were to occur exactly five years after the original investment, the mortgage balance would be $1,278,706.63, requiring the buyer to invest $921,293.37 as its equity to acquire the property and receive the benefit of the lower interest rate. An investor may be willing to do this if it has the funds available and is willing to make a 42% cash outlay for an investment property to achieve a below-market interest rate. Investor preferences, however, typically favor a lower down payment.

*Case number 3.* Assume at the time of obtaining the original mortgage, the investor was able to negotiate a mortgage that did not include a due-on-sale clause and did not prohibit additional debt secured by the property. In this case, the investor has two additional choices if the buyer wishes to leverage the property by financing 75% of the purchase price.

*Option 1.* The investor can offer to hold a standard *second mortgage* in the amount of $371,293.37 (which is the difference between the remaining balance on the original first mortgage loan and $550,000—being 25% of the purchase price—to give the buyer 75% loan to value leverage) at an agreed-upon rate close to market rates for second mortgage loans (perhaps 10.5%), amortized over an agreed-upon period (say, twenty years with a fifteen-year balloon), and the buyer can assume or take subject to the existing first mortgage-bearing interest at 6.25%. In this case, the buyer would get the benefit of the lower interest rate on the first mortgage while paying a 10.5% market rate of interest on the second mortgage; or

*Option 2.* The investor might offer the buyer a *wraparound mortgage* for the entire amount being financed ($1.65 million) at a below-market interest rate for a first mortgage loan with interest of, say, 9% on the entire amount, amortized over twenty years with a fifteen-year balloon.

If option 1 is chosen, the investor will receive at closing the sum of $550,000 in cash and will *hold paper* for $371,293.37 secured by a second mortgage, earning 10.5% interest per year, generating a monthly payment of $3,706.92, and a final balloon payment of $172,463.73 in fifteen years. The effective yield to the investor would be 10.5%.

If option 2 is chosen, the investor will receive at closing the sum of $550,000 in cash and will *hold paper* for $1.65 million bearing interest of 9% (desirable to buyer because it is 0.5% less than market and results in a monthly payment of only $14,845.48, an amount $534.68 per month less than available at the hypothetical current market rate of 9.5%). Of the $1.65 million held by the investor, only $371,293.37 represents funds actually *loaned* by the investor, which is the balance of equity the investor would have received if the property had been sold outright, without the investor providing any financing.

At first glance, it may seem that these funds will earn interest at only 9% instead of 10.5% available under option 1, but consider further: Through use of a wraparound mortgage, the investor would also earn a 2.75% return on funds of the original lender because of the spread between the 6.25% interest rate on the first mortgage loan and the 9% interest rate on the wraparound mortgage loan. Since the mortgage *wraps around* the original first mortgage loan, the balance of the wraparound mortgage amount, $1,278,706.63, represents funds actually advanced by (remaining unpaid to) the original first mortgage lender.

As a consequence, the monthly payment received on the wraparound mortgage would be $14,845.48. After payment of the underlying monthly payment of $10,963.92 due on the existing first mortgage, the net amount retained from the wraparound mortgage payment during the life of the underlying first mortgage is $3,881.56 (in this case, $174.64 per month more than the monthly payment receivable under option 1, above, with only a second mortgage position). More significantly, at the end of fifteen years, when the underlying first mortgage has been fully amortized and paid off, the balloon payment receivable under the wraparound mortgage proposed in option 2 would be $715,156.77 ($542,693.04 greater than in option 1—and, in fact, nearly double the amount originally loaned due to accumulated interest from negative amortization), generating an effective overall yield on the investor's actual cash investment of $371,293.37 at a rate of 14.32% per annum compounded monthly during the life of the loan.

Under option 2, both the investor and the buyer benefit, and the original lender continues to receive the rate of return originally contracted for under the first mortgage.

## Wrap Option Available to Banks Also

In the foregoing examples, we have assumed that it is the investor/seller who is providing the financing and who will be the *wraparound mortgagee*. This is not necessarily the case. There is no legal reason a bank or other lender could not be the wraparound mortgagee under similar circumstances provided it is not prohibited by regulatory mandate or internal loan policies from securing loans through use of a *junior mortgage*.

In this case, the transaction would be structured by having the bank be the wraparound lender. The bank would advance to the buyer the additional $371,293.37 needed to pay off the seller as a loan secured by a wraparound mortgage. The buyer would contribute $550,000 as 25% of the purchase price; the bank would lend the buyer an additional $371,293.37, taking back a wraparound mortgage for $1.65 million (75% of the purchase price). At closing, the investor/seller would receive its entire equity of

$921,293.37, and the original lender would continue to carry its first mortgage with a principal balance of $1,278,706.63 at 6.25% for the balance of fifteen years.

Except for substitution of the bank in place of the investor as the wraparound mortgagee, all other loan attributes remain the same: the buyer gets the benefit of below-market interest (9% instead of 9.5%); the seller receives all its equity to invest or use as the seller determines appropriate; the original lender continues to receive the benefit of its contracted for fixed interest rate over the term of its loan; and the bank, as wraparound mortgagee, receives an effective interest yield of 14.32%. Everyone wins.

## Potential Legal Advantages and Documentation

In addition to the yield enhancement benefits enjoyed by the wraparound lender, another advantage of a wraparound mortgage as compared with a simple *second mortgage* is that the collateral priority of a wraparound mortgage may, over time, migrate to a collateral priority on par with the first mortgage.

For the most part, a wraparound mortgage should mirror the provisions of the senior mortgage around which it *wraps* with a pass through to the mortgagor of virtually all mortgagor covenants. An essential element of a wraparound mortgage, however, is that it must require the borrower to make all payments to the wraparound mortgagee, who will, in turn, be obligated to pay the senior mortgagee. The wraparound mortgage and related documentation must not permit the mortgagor to pay the first mortgagee directly. It is this arrangement that, legally, may enhance the wraparound mortgagee's collateral position.

Although not entirely clear from reported-case law, at least one respected commentator has suggested that this migration of lien priority is a natural consequence of applicable subrogation law. Judicial interpretation of this proposition in the context of wraparound mortgages, however, has been scant and, in most jurisdictions, nonexistent.

While this legal position appears sound in circumstances where the indebtedness secured by a superior lien is paid in full (see *Aames Capital Corporation v. Interstate Bank of Lake Forest*, 312 Ill. App. 3d 700 [(2nd Dist., 2000] and *LaSalle Bank, N.A. v. First American Bank*, 316 Ill. App. 3d 515 [1st Dist., 2000]), its application to partial payments under a wraparound mortgage with pro rata subrogation remains largely untested.

Still, building a case for preservation of this outcome is desirable. Accordingly, the wraparound mortgage and supporting documentation should include covenants of subrogation to establish the clear intent of the parties that subrogation to the lien of the senior loan is to occur with each payment by the wraparound mortgagee to the senior lender. By inclusion of specific language to this effect, the doctrine of *conventional subrogation* may be sufficient to achieve this result. The doctrine of conventional subrogation is discussed by John C. Murray in his article "Equitable and Conventional Subrogation in Illinois" published in 2003 and available through First American Title Company (*www.firstam.com*).

From an underwriting standpoint, however, until this issue is definitively settled through judicial interpretation or otherwise, it is appropriate to analyze a proposed loan secured by a wraparound mortgage as being a loan secured by a junior mortgage.

Some commentators have raised the additional issue of whether future payments by a wraparound mortgagee to a senior lender enjoy priority over liens filed subsequent to the date of recording a wraparound mortgage but prior to the date of payment of future installments to the senior lender. This issue is implicated because most wraparound mortgages provide that the wraparound mortgagee is required to pay the senior lender only to the extent of funds actually received from the wraparound mortgagor, giving rise to the legal dichotomy between obligatory future advances and nonobligatory future advances.

The prevailing view is that this issue is adequately resolved through conventional subrogation and through the rule of *tacking*, which provides that a mortgagee who pays a prior encumbrance (whether or not subrogation applies) is entitled to include such amount in the indebtedness secured by the lien of its mortgage. (See *McCormick v Knox, 105 U.S. 122 [1881]; Harper v. Ely, 70 Ill. 581 [1873]; Boone v. Clark, 129 Ill. 466 (1889); Black's Law Dictionary, 6th ed.,* definition of *tacking,* West Publishing Company, St. Paul, Minnesota.)

Other covenants are useful or necessary to preserve the yield enhancement provided by use of a wraparound mortgage. In particular, a covenant in the wraparound mortgage that the underlying first mortgage may not be prepaid by the wraparound mortgagor is essential since it is the interest rate spread between the wraparound mortgage and the underlying first mortgage that enhances the effective yield to the wraparound mortgagee. Also, a cross-default provision in the wraparound mortgage, providing that a default under the senior mortgage will constitute a material default under the wraparound mortgage, is a useful protective covenant.

Proper documentation of a loan secured by a wraparound mortgage loan is critical to maximize the potential benefits and afford the legal protections a wraparound mortgage may provide.

## Advanced Planning Is the Key

Wraparound mortgages are useful legal devices that seldom arise except during periods of rising interest rates. When interest rates rise, wraparound mortgages provide a legally sound tool for preserving the benefits of long-term low interest rate loans. Not only do they enable investors and banks to realize enhanced effective yields on commercial real estate loans, they can also make properties and loans more marketable by enabling the buyer to pay a lower overall interest rate than may otherwise be generally available in the marketplace.

To take advantage of the benefits of a wraparound mortgage when interest rates rise, the investor/borrower must plan now, while long-term interest rates are low, by negotiating loan terms that facilitate their use. Key among these provisions are elimination or limitation of the due-on-sale clause and elimination or limitation of a negative borrowing covenant that prevents the property from securing other indebtedness. Similarly, all other provisions of the mortgage loan must be carefully reviewed with an eye toward future use of a wraparound mortgage to protect against unforeseen obstacles.

With proper planning and effective negotiation at the time of obtaining a low-interest, long-term loan secured by investment real estate, a wraparound mortgage may provide a unique opportunity to profit when interest rates rise.

# 26

# Mind Your Contacts

Commercial real estate is a relationship business. You must pay attention to your business contacts and help them when you can. Do not let too much time pass without at least sending them a note or giving them a call or sending them a referral to remind them you are thinking of them. This will help them think of you.

Virtually every project and every transaction involves a team of participants in addition to the seller, purchaser, and/or developer.

The seller's team will typically include, at least, a commercial real estate broker, a commercial real estate transaction attorney, a title insurance agent, a surveyor, and an accountant, tax attorney, or other tax advisor.

The purchaser's team will typically include, at least, a commercial real estate broker, a commercial real estate transaction attorney, a tax advisor, an environmental consultant, and perhaps an environmental lawyer.

A developer's team will often include a commercial real estate broker, commercial real estate transaction attorney, and environmental consultant, as well as engineers, project managers, marketing managers, sale or leasing agents, financial analysts and consultants, and perhaps zoning and entitlement counsel, who may or may not be the same attorney as the commercial real estate transaction counsel.

In any given transaction or project, there may be a multitude of other professions involved on each team. Typically, there is a *team leader* who serves as the *point person* to oversee and coordinate the team to make sure the transaction or project proceeds on schedule and as planned.

Who are the team leaders? Most often, the team leader is the project manager for the purchaser, seller, or developer (which may be the same person as the purchaser, seller, or developer) or its transaction attorney. Other team members may influence the team leader and suggest alternatives, but the team leader typically decides whom he or she will work with.

Understand that any commercial real estate professional serving as a team leader has a huge number of choices as to whom to place on his or her team. It is likely that team leaders will repeatedly turn to the people they know and trust unless something happens to make that person not available or to make the team leader less than entirely satisfied with a prior experience. This is to be expected, since responsibility for completing most aspects of the transaction or project rests with the designated team leader.

I have my own set of A-list team members. My A-list is comprised of commercial real estate professionals who are skilled, responsive, easy to work with, and who consistently deliver value. Each has their own area of expertise. They are all very good at what they do. When the opportunity arises, I highly recommend them to my clients and to others.

To assist you in your quest to prosper in commercial real estate, I have listed some of my A-list team members and their current contact information below. Since the list is constantly evolving, I will keep it updated under the appropriate tab at *www.intenttoprosper.com*. If you find the opportunity to use them, do so with confidence, and please tell them I referred you.

# Recommended Real Estate Professionals
## R. Kymn Harp's A-list (2009-2010)

**Financial Consultants/Receivers**
**Asset Managers—Distressed Properties**

**High Ridge Partners Inc.**
**Attn: Nancy A. Ross, Tina L. Hughes**
**Mike Eber, and James Busk**
140 S Dearborn St. # 420
Chicago IL 60603
Telephone 312-456-5636
*www.high-ridge.com*

**DSI—Development Specialists Inc.**
**Attn: John C. Wheeler**
Three First National Plaza
70 West Madison St.
Suite 2300
Chicago IL 60602-4250
Telephone 312-263-4141
*www.dsi.biz*

**Rally Capital Services LLC**
**Attn: Steve Baer**
350 North LaSalle St.
Suite 1100
Chicago IL 60654
Telephone 312-661-0644
*www.rallyllc.com*

**Foresite Realty Partners LLC**
**Attn: Donald Shapiro and Jamie Hadac**
6400 Shafer Court
Rosemont IL 60018
Telephone 847-939-6010
*www.foresiterealty.com*

## Investment Bankers

**Dresner Partners**
**Steven M. Dresner and Gregg D. Pollack**
20 N. Clark St., Suite 3550
Chicago IL 60602
Telephone 312-726-3600
*www.dresnerpartners.com*

**Dougherty & Company LLC**
**Attn: Walter "Wally" C. Parkins**
90 South Seventh St.
Suite 4400
Minneapolis MN 55402-4115
Telephone 612-376-4137
*www.doughertymarkets.com*

## Commercial-Industrial Real Estate Brokers

**Jones Lang LaSalle Americas, Inc.**
**Trevor Ragsdale and Len Caldeira**
200 East Randolph Street, Floor 47
Chicago, Illinois 60601
Telephone 312-782-5800
Trevor Ragsdale Dir. 312-228-3092
Len Caldeira Dir. 312-228-3958
*www.joneslanglasalle.com*

**Millennium Properties R/E Inc.**
**Attn. Daniel J. Hyman**
Two First National Plaza
20 S. Clark St., Suite 630
Chicago IL 60602
Telephone 312-338-3000
*www.mpirealestate.com*

## Multifamily Asset Management and LIHTC

**AIMCO Capital**
**Attn: Chris Podraza**
1801 S. Meyers Rd., Suite 300
Oakbrook Terrace IL 60181
Telephone 630-812-2159
*www.aimco.com*

## Multifamily Distressed Property—Private Equity Fund

**US Residential, LLC**
**Attn: T. J. Wojtas**
39 S. LaSalle St., Suite 1400
Chicago, IL 60603
Telephone 312-784-7100.
*www.usresidential.com*

## Commercial—Office Property Management

**Lieberman Management Services Inc.**
**Attn: Stanley B. Lieberman and Jim Pio**
355 W. Dundee Rd.
Buffalo Grove IL 60089
Telephone 847-777-7700
*www.liebermanmanagement.com*

## Environmental Consultants

**Apex Companies Inc.**
**Attn: Steve Torres**
531 W. Golf Rd.
Arlington Heights IL 60005
Telephone 847-956-8589 x 204
*www.apexcos.com*

**EPI—Environmental Protection Industries Inc.**
**Attn: Joseph Musa**
16650 South Canal
South Holland IL 60473
Telephone 708-225-1115
*www.environmental-epi.com*

**The Payne Firm Inc.**
**Attn: Howard J. Zwirn**
325 West Huron St.
Suite 410
Chicago IL 60610
Telephone 800-229-1443
*www.paynefirm.com*

## Title Insurance

**Lawyers Title Insurance Company**
**Commonwealth Land Title Insurance Company**
**Attn: Lisa Metzler**
10 South LaSalle St., Suite 2500
Chicago, IL 60603
Telephone (312) 601-6591
*www.landam.com*

**TICOR Title Insurance Co.**
**Attn: Shari L. Haefner**
National Commercial Services
203. N. LaSalle St.
Chicago IL 60601
Telephone 312-621-5020
*www.illinois.ticortitle.com/sections/NatCommercial.asp*

**Chicago Title Insurance Company**
**Attn: Allison F. Rabin**
171 N. Clark St.—ML02LT
Chicago, IL 60601
Telephone (312) 223-2230
*www.ctic.com*

**First American Title Insurance Company**
**Attn: Steven I. Zellinger**
National Commercial Services
30 North LaSalle St., Suite 310
Chicago, IL 60602
Telephone 312-917-7257
*szellinger@firstam.com*
*www.firstam.com*

## *Section 1031 Exchange Services*

**Chicago Deferred Exchange Company**
**Naomi Weitzel**
Senior Vice President
135 South LaSalle Street, Suite 1940
Chicago, IL 60603
**Telephone: (312) 580-9603**
*naomi.weitzel@cdec1031.com*

## *Design-Build Developers*

**Ryan Companies US Inc.—Naperville IL**
**Attn: Jeff A. Smith and Tim Hennelly**
55 Shuman Blvd.
Suite 800
Naperville IL 60563
Telephone 630-328-1100
*www.ryancompanies.com*

**Ryan Companies US Inc.—Minneapolis MN**
**Attn: Tim Gray**
50 South 10th St., Suite 300
Minneapolis MN 55403
Telephone 612-492-4000
*www.ryancompanies.com*

**Leopardo Companies Inc.**
**Attn: J. Casey Kahler**
5200 Prairie Stone Pkwy.
Hoffman Estates IL 60192
Telephone 847-783-3314
*www.leopardo.com*

## *Property Preservation, Inspection, and Rehab*

**Fast Securing Inc.**
**Attn: Orville E. Frame, Jr.**
925 W 171st St.
East Hazel Crest IL 60429
Telephone 708-799-0700
*www.fastsecuring.com*

## Technology Products and Services

### CDW Corporation
### Attn: Ryan Harp
Account Manager
(Woodland Falls)
26125 N. Riverwoods Blvd.
Mettawa IL 60045
Telephone 847-371-7181
*www.cdw.com*

## Marketing Consultants

### AKINA Corporation
### Attn: Deborah Knupp
40 E. Chicago Ave, Suite 166
Chicago IL 60611
Telephone 312-235-0144
*www.akina.biz*

## Project Branding

### Porter Specialty Advertising Corporation
### Attn: Kery M. Wirth
463 W. Fullerton Ave.
Elmhurst, IL 60126
Telephone 630-833-1630
Mobile 847-903-0835
*kerypie@gmail.com*
*www.porterspecialty.com*

*Architectural Photography*

**Steven Dahlman Photography**
**Attn: Steven Dahlman**
300 North State St.
Chicago IL 60654
Telephone 312-644-6260
*www.stevendahlman.com*

If you have worked on a transaction or development team, stay in touch with your team members. Give them a reason to include you on the next project or transaction and to refer you to others. If you become aware that you are not always on the team leader's *A-list*, keep at it. Teams change. If the team leader's A-list team member filling your position becomes unavailable or if the team leader becomes disenchanted with that member, you want to be first in the team leader's mind to serve as a replacement.

When I serve as a team leader, I am like all other team leaders. I tend to use the people I know and trust. I want people on my team who are competent, pleasant to work with, and dependable.

You will also want to be sure you get value for the money you commit to team members. Hiring team members from the largest and best-known companies and firms may not be your best choice. You need competence and experience, but you probably don't need the inflated prices of large firms unless you get genuine value in return. This goes for architectural firms, accounting firms, law firms, commercial/industrial real estate brokers, financial consultants, environmental consultants, and most other professions.

*Case in point*: In March 2008, I decided to move my practice to a 30-lawyer law firm from a 150-lawyer firm. As you may know, these are trying times for law firms. Clients, more than ever, are demanding value. Previously perceived *prestige value* associated with the biggest and most expensive law firms has, for commercial real estate development, investment, and financing, been supplanted by a demand for superior *economic value*. The time had come to lose the bulk and become part of a lean, efficient, value driven team.

I had good years at my old law firm. Good lawyers and good friends. But times have changed. Sometimes less is more.

Don't get me wrong. There is a time and place for large law firms. It's just that for me—and for my clients—*now* is *not* that time.

My clients don't need multiple offices in sunbelt retirement communities. It may be nice for the old guys ready to retire, but we're a long way from that.

My clients also don't need sixteen teams of ten lawyers each to change a lightbulb.

For commercial real estate investment, finance, and development, how many lawyers do you need? Even the most sophisticated commercial real estate transactions seldom need more than two or three lawyers and a paralegal. For most, one lawyer will do and is more efficient and cost effective. If a commercial real estate project is getting touched by six, eight, or ten lawyers, each billing at premium rates, you have to ask yourself, is this really necessary? How much duplication is going on? How many lawyers need to learn the same facts and review the same documents? At what cost? Is the client really getting value for its legal dollars?

If a client believes the answer is "yes, it's worth the excess cost," that's the client's call. Clients are free to spend their money however they wish.

I can only tell you this: I have been closing commercial real estate transactions and handling commercial real estate financing and development for over thirty years. The last five years were at a large law firm. At Robbins, Salomon & Patt Ltd., my billing rate is 20% less. The quality isn't less—our overhead is less. The difference is clear.

As I said, there is a time and place for hiring a large law firm and paying premium rates. The question to ask, is this that time or place?

The usual pitch from large law firms is that they have one-hundred-plus trial lawyers, five or six tax lawyers, two dozen business lawyers, and ten or so real estate lawyers, as well as several others. That's nice. If you're a commercial real estate investor, developer, or lender, do you really need one hundred trial lawyers? If you are involved in that much litigation, shouldn't you be looking for other answers?

Who do you think is paying for all those lawyers and their paralegals and their staff and their office space and their insurance premiums and the retirement accounts to keep them in those cushy sunbelt offices when they're not out playing golf? You think it's their *other* clients?

I really don't mean this as an indictment against large law firms. They have their place. Exxon Mobil needs them. Cardinal Health needs them. Apparently, ATA, Aloha, Skybus, and Frontier airlines need them. The question is, do you need them? That is a question only each client can answer.

According to many MBAs, the bottom-line margin of profit in most industries is around 5%. At that rate, it takes a $1 million increase in gross revenue to net $50,000. Another way to net $50,000 is to reduce costs by that much. If you can do so without sacrificing quality or responsiveness, why not?

I'm not pointing this out simply because I decided to move to a smaller, more efficient law firm. I decided to move to a smaller, more efficient law firm because my clients and I recognized this reality.

Clients rely on their attorneys to act in the clients' best interest. Attorneys owe a fiduciary duty to their clients. That does not just mean providing the highest possible quality of service, although it certainly means that. It also includes making a serious evaluation of whether clients are getting full value for their legal fee dollars.

There is a basic philosophical divide. It is centered in the debate over whether the practice of law is a business or a profession. In reality, it is both. The issue is one of balance. The predominant view seems to be to charge the most money possible for legal services rendered. The better view is to deliver the best legal services possible for the legal fees we receive. A true distinction with a difference.

The point of this is that you should demand quality and value from those who serve you, and you must deliver quality and value to those you serve. Whatever your role, you are on the team because the team leader has determined your skill set is needed. Do your part timely, effectively, and with enthusiasm, for a fair price. This is the only surefire road to prosperity in commercial real estate. If you intend to prosper, begin and make it happen.

# 27

# Parting Shot

Commercial real estate is my passion. It always has been. I find everything about it exciting. Development. Acquisition. Sale. Financing. Project entitlement. Loan workouts. You name it. If it relates to commercial real estate, I'm interested.

I have friends who marvel at the great mountains of Colorado and beyond. Mountains are certainly majestic, spiritual, and powerful. I understand the attraction. But it is a well-developed city skyline that gets my juices flowing. The skylines of Chicago and Manhattan and other great cities are my mountains.

I love Chicago largely because Chicago is a great real estate town. This is a wonderful place to be in the real estate industry. Come to Chicago and take a skyline tour along the Lake Michigan lakefront, or cruise on one of the ninety-minute architectural tours on the Chicago River through downtown Chicago. They are fascinating to anyone interested in architecture and commercial real estate development.

I am always looking for new projects, new experiences, and new challenges in commercial real estate. New projects are my lifeblood. The more challenging, the better. If you have a commercial real estate project and need a project team leader or simply the help of an experienced and enthusiastic commercial real estate attorney, I hope you will call me. Not only will we have fun, but every project teaches a new lesson. The lessons we learn together will form the basis of *Intent to Prosper, Vol. 2.*

You can contact me through *www.rsplaw.com*, or *www.intenttoprosper.com* or *www.realestate-law.com*. If a project comes up and you cannot remember these Web sites, just Google my name, R. Kymn Harp.

As you find a need for high-quality real estate professionals to fill out your project teams, do not hesitate to use the companies and people I have referred to and recommended in this book. Others will be added to my A-list of recommended real estate professionals maintained at the *www. intenttoprosper.com* Web site as circumstances warrant.

I invite you also to submit your questions and comments and project descriptions through *www.intenttoprosper.com*. I am always interested. When valuable lessons can be taught, I will seek your permission to post them on the Web site and may highlight them in the next volume of *Intent to Prosper.*

Hopefully, we will work together soon. Until then, enjoy yourself, be healthy, and prosper.

Thank you for taking the time to read this book.

# INDEX